Also by Richard J. Brenner

THE WORLD SERIES, The Great Contests
THE COMPLETE SUPER BOWL STORY
JOHN ELWAY * BERNIE KOSAR
ROGER CLEMENS * DARRYL STRAWBERRY

MICHAEL JORDAN * MAGIC JOHNSON

RICHARD J. BRENNER

EAST END PUBLISHING
New York

Dedication

For Anita, my wife and research chief. To Halle and Jason, two wonderful children, two wonderful people, thank you for your help, your time, your encouragement, and your patience.

And to Marvin Gluckman and Jerry Geller, the best friends that I have ever had. I hope that your lives are filled with beauty and joy.

Special thanks to: Chris Kingsley of Lynx Communications, Joyce Mead of SportsChrome, and Joyce Szymanski of the Chicago Bulls. And most of all to Bette Lipsky and Barry Varela.

And for my mother, who has given me life and love.

JORDON * JOHNSON

ISBN: 0-943403-04-9

First Printing/February 1989
Revised October 1989

Photo Credits

Cover Photos: Front cover: Noren Trotman/Sportschrome
Back cover: Jordan—Noren Trotman/Sportschrome
Back cover: Johnson—Brian Drake/Sportschrome
Interior Photos

Michael Jordan photos: The Olympic photo: Courtesy of the Chicago Bulls
All other Jordan photos: Bill Smith, Courtesy of the Chicago Bulls

Magic Johnson: Photo from Michigan State: Courtesy of
Michigan State University
All other Magic Johnson shots: UPI/Bettmann Newsphotos

Printed in the United States of America

The author wishes to acknowledge the following:

Scott Ostler and Steve Springer, *Winnin' Times*
James Haskins, *Magic: A Biography of Earvin Johnson.*
Gary Burchard, *Magic Johnson*
Bruce Weber, *Magic Johnson—Larry Bird*
The Sporting News
Newsweek
Sport Magazine
Sports Illustrated
Detroit News
The New York Times
The Los Angeles Times
Current Biography Yearbook

MICHAEL JORDAN

1

In the Beginning

Before anyone knew that he would be able to "fly," the man that millions of fans around the world would come to know as Air Jordan was simply named Michael Jeffrey Jordan.

Michael was born February 17, 1963, in Brooklyn, New York. He was the third child in a family that would eventually grow to five children.

When Michael was still a youngster, his parents, James and Delores, moved the family to Wilmington, North Carolina. And it was there, along with his brothers, Larry and James, and his sisters, Delores and Roslyn, that Michael grew up.

James, who worked as a supervisor in a General Electric plant, and Delores, who worked as a customer-service supervisor at a bank, gave their children a good home, a strong sense of family, and the security of being loved.

The Jordans always taught their children that they must strive to reach their goals. As James puts it, "The way it is in our family is that we try to make something happen rather than waiting around for it to happen. We believe the surest way is to work toward making it the way you want it." James modestly gives Delores all the credit for Michael's drive to the top in athletics. "Michael got his competitive nature from his mother. She's a winner."

James can definitely take the credit for another Jordan trademark, though—the famous tongue-wagging. Millions of basketball fans all around the world have seen the pictures of Michael intensely gliding through defenders or arching a jump shot toward the hoop with his tongue hanging out of his mouth. Michael picked up the habit from watching his dad stick out his tongue as he worked around the house.

But the most important heritage that Michael received from his parents was a loving family, constant support and encourage-

3

ment, and the realization that rewards are the desserts of effort. Michael's parents were always there to cheer his efforts, and they made it their business to attend most of his games—from Little League through college. But before Michael got to bounce the ball, he had to do all the chores that were assigned to him. First he had to be disciplined and make his contribution, and only then was it time for the games to begin.

James and Delores knew that it takes self-discipline to be successful in life, and they also knew that there are dangers lurking in some dark corners. Michael still remembers their lessons. "My parents warned me about the traps. The drugs and drink, the streets that could catch you if you got careless. I was lazy about some things. I never got into mowing the lawn or doing hard jobs. But I wasn't careless."

After watching Michael soar above the hoop as gracefully as an eagle in the sky, it's hard to believe that he hasn't always moved so naturally and gracefully or that basketball wasn't his first love.

While Michael was growing up, he played all of the major sports, but baseball was his favorite. In Little League he showed a lively arm and tossed two no-hitters.

When Michael was thirteen, James built a backyard basketball court, and Michael and his older brother Larry and their friends played on it almost every day. Larry at the time was the taller of the two boys, so when they went one-on-one, Michael had to play harder to try to stay even. His hustling won him the nickname of Rabbit.

When Michael entered Laney High School, though, his hustle couldn't make up for his lack of experience, and he failed to make the varsity as a freshman. In his second year Michael made the varsity briefly but was cut early in the season.

But Michael wouldn't quit. He just dug in his heels and worked that much harder. Nearly every day the thump of the basketball could be heard on the backyard court as he and Larry went one-on-one.

Michael remembers those backyard duels with great fondness and admiration for his older brother. "Larry always used to beat me on the backyard court. His vertical jump is higher than mine.

4

He's got the dunks and some three-sixties and most of all the same stuff I have. And he's only five-seven! He's my inspiration."

Michael played some varsity football, and he was also on the track team, where he specialized in—what else?—the long jump and the high jump. But at the time it seemed that baseball would be the sport where Michael would make his mark. He hadn't yet shown any exceptional talent on the basketball court, and no one in his family, including his dad, was six feet tall.

But the constant practice with Larry improved his skills, and a growth spurt that saw Michael soar from five feet eleven inches to six-three between his sophomore and junior years took care of the height situation. When the basketball season began, Michael was ready.

The Jordan brothers gave the Laney High School basketball team a dynamic duo, and the entire clan came out to cheer. Because he liked and respected Larry so much, Michael chose twenty-three for his uniform number, which was as close as he could get to one-half of Larry's forty-five.

During the summer Clifton Herring, the basketball coach at Laney, used his influence to get Michael into Howie Garfinkel's Five Star Basketball Camp in Pittsburgh. The camp is an intense training ground as well as a showcase for big-time college prospects. Being at the camp made Michael feel "as though someone had tapped me on the shoulder with a magic wand and said, 'You must emerge as somebody—somebody to be admired, to achieve big things. But don't lose your identity.'"

Michael never had to worry about forgetting who he was or where he came from. He is the same caring, considerate person today as he was back in high school. The big difference is that today Michael is no longer the shy youngster who couldn't communicate with girls and who thought of himself as a "gooney."

Throughout Michael's senior year at Laney, Coach Herring, who lived a block away from the Jordans, would pick Michael up at six every morning so that he could have an extra hour of basketball practice.

The practice paid big dividends. Michael, who made many

high school all-American teams after his senior season, received interest from many big-time college basketball powers.

Michael didn't have to look very far to find a college that could provide a good education and a first-rate basketball program. The state of North Carolina has an abundance of colleges that would have fit the bill, including such perennial Atlantic Coast Conference basketball powers as Duke University, the University of North Carolina, and North Carolina State University.

Michael's mom was a big fan of the Tar Heels, so she favored the University of North Carolina. And its basketball program is coached by Dean Smith, widely considered to be one of the very best coaches in the country.

The choice seemed obvious, except for one little problem. "Growing up," recalls Michael, "I hated North Carolina. I was an NC State fan. David Thompson was the man. [Thompson was a college all-American who went on to become an NBA All-Star.] My mom liked Phil Ford [an all-American at the University of North Carolina who went on to a fine pro career], but I couldn't stand him or any of those UNC guys. I even rooted for Marquette to beat the Tar Heels in the 1977 NCAA championship game. My mom got mad at that."

But Michael's hate turned to something else when he made an unannounced visit to the UNC campus at Chapel Hill. "The coaches didn't even know I was there. I saw the place as a student, not as a recruit." That visit was enough to convince Michael that UNC was the place for him. It also made his mom and Tar Heel Coach Dean Smith very happy.

During the summer after his senior year, Michael attended Coach Smith's summer basketball camp. Michael learned a lot of basketball and met Buzz Peterson, another hoopster who was about to enter UNC. The two young men quickly became friends, and so did their families. According to James Jordan, "It's a beautiful friendship. From the first time we met Buzz's parents, we hit it off. They're likable and easy to know. We've always looked on Michael's friends as our sons, and we advise them as we do Michael."

What made this relationship just a little bit unusual—and a good lesson for people everywhere—is that the Jordans are black and the Petersons are white. The two families, obviously, were more interested in character and personality than in skin tones.

Michael was also happy about the fact that Roslyn, his younger sister, had skipped her last year at Laney and would also be attending UNC. Happily for Michael, he had a new friend and a sister to make him feel a little bit at home on campus. Now all he had to do was start taking college courses and try to play his way onto a team that had gone to the finals of the NCAA championship the preceding spring.

2

Superman

Michael and Buzz decided to become roommates, and they also decided to limit their social activities so that they could focus their efforts on their schoolwork and basketball. Part of their spare time was spent by Michael teaching Buzz how to shoot pool and by Buzz teaching Michael how to play golf, which would become an ongoing passion for Michael.

"What impressed me most about Michael," Peterson recalls, "was his love for his family. And he was a fun guy to be around. All that ends when he goes on the court, though. Then he becomes deadly serious."

Michael used that intensity, a lot of hard work, and his blossoming talent to become the only freshman starter on a power-packed team that was anchored in the frontcourt by all-Americans James Worthy (currently with the LA Lakers) and Sam Perkins (now with the Dallas Mavericks).

Michael, playing in the backcourt and at small forward, helped UNC post a spectacular 23–2 record. He averaged a respectable 13.5 points and four rebounds per game. More importantly, though, he demonstrated a knack for making the big play when it was needed most, and his overall performance earned him the selection as the Atlantic Coast Conference's Rookie of the Year. What made UNC's record especially impressive is the fact that it was achieved largely against teams from the ACC, which is consistently one of the two or three top conferences in college basketball.

UNC's record earned them a place in the 1982 NCAA tournament. They won the East finals and then traveled on to New Orleans for the Final Four, the World Series and Super Bowl of college basketball. The Tar Heels beat a very talented Houston team in the semi-finals, and then it was showdown time against Patrick Ewing and the Georgetown Hoyas. Coach John

Thompson's Georgetown team was considered to be one of the finest and most aggressive college hoop squads of all time, and Ewing was judged to be the most dominant college center in the past thirty years. It looked as though it was going to be another disappointing finale for Dean Smith, who had been hailed as a great coach and had won many awards but never the national title.

The matchup turned out to be everything that a fan could want in a championship game. The two teams went toe-to-toe, trading baskets in front of a wildly cheering overflow crowd at the Superdome and a national TV audience. With less than a minute left to play, UNC took possession of the ball, trailing by 62–61. They worked the ball around, hoping to go inside to James Worthy. Worthy did get the pass, but he was covered and kicked the ball back out to where Michael was. There were sixteen seconds left as Michael took the ball, leaped up, and swished a seventeen-foot jump shot through the net to give UNC the win 63–62.

Dean Smith finally had the missing jewel in his coaching crown after coming up empty for 24 years at UNC. He was thrilled by the stunning victory and appreciative of Michael's last-second heroics. "I've seen other great athletes," said Coach Smith of the player that fans and teammates had nicknamed Superman, "but Michael has the intelligence, the court savvy, and the burning desire—a dedication. He was a hero so many times at the end of games—it was uncanny. It really was."

Michael's shot capped a storybook freshman season that saw him propelled to a place among the legends of college basketball. In addition to being named the ACC Rookie of the Year, he had been selected for the all-tournament teams in the postseason ACC tournament and the Final Four of the NCAA tournament. And the folks back home were so thrilled by the championship that had been so elusive, that the telephone company that services the Chapel Hill area put a picture of Michael taking the final shot on the front cover of the phone book.

When Michael returned for his sophomore year and the 1982–83 basketball season, he knew that he and Sam Perkins were being counted on as the mainstays of the team. James

Worthy, the all-American forward, had decided to leave school the previous spring to pursue a professional career and accept the financial security of a long-term, big-bucks contract with the Los Angeles Lakers.

Michael responded to the challenge by raising the level of his game on offense as well as defense. On offense his scoring average zoomed to twenty points a game, which was good enough to lead the ACC, despite the fact that he was usually double-teamed. Michael had worked on and improved his outside shot, which made it that much harder for defenders to play off him and defense the drive. But when a defender came up to try to stop the jump shot, Michael could begin his dribble, accelerate past his man, spin around the double-team, explode into the air or soar above the basket like a bird in flight, and slam the ball down through the net. Michael's ability to hit the jump shot, coupled with his incomparable move to the hoop, gave coaches night-mares and demoralized defenders. As Maryland's star guard Adrian Branch put it, "Guarding Jordan is dirty, dirty work."

And on the other end of the floor, Michael, through constant practice, developed into a devastating defensive performer who could turn a game around with a key steal or blocked shot. He was very proud of his defensive play, which eliminated what had been the one weak link in his game.

Coach Smith had known that with Michael's quickness, athlet-icism, and court sense he could, with hard work, become a dominant defensive player. Coach Smith put Michael's abilities to their best use by making him a "roamer," which gave him the option of leaving the player he was guarding to go for the ball—like a free safety in football—whenever he saw an oppor-tunity.

Michael wound up with 78 steals, an average of more than two per game, the second-highest single-season total in UNC history. And he handled his assignment so well and worked so hard that he wound up with 12 defensive game awards after failing to win even one as a freshman.

Michael's efforts were rewarded when he was unanimously voted to the all-American squad and selected as *The Sporting News* College Player of the Year. In its explanation of the award,

The Sporting News noted, "He soars through the air, he rebounds, he scores [more than 1,100 points in two years, a school record], he guards two men at once, he blocks shots, he makes steals. More important, he makes late plays that win games."

During the summer between his sophomore and junior years, Michael sharpened his skills by touring the globe with several all-star teams. Later on that summer he led the United States team to a gold medal at the Pan-American Games in Caracas, Venezuela. The Pan-American Games are like a mini-Olympics that bring together in competition the best amateur athletes in North and South America.

Michael enjoyed traveling to other countries and making friends with people from different parts of the world. And Michael, with his quick smile and friendly nature, made friends wherever he went. As Michael's mom said, "Michael never really meets a stranger." Michael liked traveling so much that he made geography his major at UNC.

When September rolled around, Michael was back in Chapel Hill, ready to hit the books and crash the boards. He showed just how ready he was, as he along with Sam Perkins led the Tar Heels to a first-place finish in the ACC. And once again Michael's amazing all-around play earned him *The Sporting News* College Player of the Year award. Mike Douchant, an editor at *The Sporting News,* explained why. "Jordan . . . went to the top of the class because of the frequency with which he produced in clutch situations. Sometimes Jordan spontaneously performs an electrifying high-wire act. Sometimes he puts his acrobatic assaults on hold and simply glides in for a layup or pulls up for a soft jumper. On other occasions, Jordan improvises and assumes control of a game with a crucial steal or blocked shot."

The Tar Heels rode their first-place finish in the ACC to a trip to the NCAA tournament. But the train got only as far as the Eastern semi-finals before it was derailed by the Bobby Knight–coached Indiana Hoosiers, 72–68. Nobody realized it at the time, but that would turn out to be the last performance that Michael would give in the powder-blue uniform of UNC.

After the season Michael decided that he would leave school at the end of his junior year to play in the NBA. He had nothing left to prove in the college game, and he knew that if he came back, he would be a marked man. He would constantly be going up against double- and triple-teaming and zone defenses designed to slow the tempo of his game. Staying at the college level would only slow his development as a basketball player. And there was always the risk of serious injury that could deprive Michael of the security of the long-term guaranteed contract that he was sure to be offered for turning pro. Both his parents and Coach Smith agreed with Michael's decision, especially after he told them that he would return to UNC in the off-seasons to continue his studies and earn his degree.

Michael was the third selection in the NBA's annual draft of college players, behind two seven-footers, Akeem Olajuwon of the University of Houston and Sam Bowie of the University of Kentucky. That two teams passed over Michael caused a stirring among knowledgeable basketball people. One could make a strong case for Houston's selection of Akeem "The Dream," who was a hometown hero and a center with extraordinary potential. But even given the fact that NBA teams prefer to build their squads around large centers rather than forwards or guards, the choice of Bowie by the Portland Trail Blazers seemed curious. Dirk Minnifield, a close friend of Bowie's and a fine basketball player, summed up the thoughts of a lot of people when he said, "Houston and Portland are both going to be sorry they didn't draft him." The fans in Chicago sure weren't sorry though. They were thrilled that Michael would be coming to the Windy City to play for the Bulls.

Before joining the NBA, though, Michael's itinerary called for a stop in Los Angeles to represent the United States in the 1984 Summer Olympics. It was an opportunity that Michael cherished.

Basketball watchers were curious to see how Michael and Bobby Knight, who had been selected to be the head coach of the Olympic team, would work together.

Michael had been superbly coached and taught to play structured basketball at a high level at UNC. But because of his enormous abilities and court savvy, he had been permitted to play a freewheeling game within Coach Smith's system.

12

Coach Knight has a reputation as a strict disciplinarian who insists upon everything being done his way. Knight, unlike Dean Smith, is a hothead who screams at his players. He has also been known to throw chairs as well as tantrums.

What would happen, people wondered, when the irrepressible player collided with the immovable coach? What would happen when Michael took the ball and launched himself into orbit to create a play that neither Knight nor anyone else had designed?

"The first few times he did that on the Olympic team," according to an assistant coach, "Coach Knight would stop practice and explain to him why it was wrong. But then we noticed that he could hang in the air for so long and do so many things with the ball that he was almost always successful. So we stopped coaching him after that."

Michael, though, kept playing, and he and Patrick Ewing led the US squad into the finals against the team from Spain, a team they had trounced 101–68 in the opening round of the competition. The United States team played relentlessly during the final game and romped to a 32-point victory and the Olympic gold medal. After the game a frustrated but admiring Spanish coach exclaimed about Michael, "He's not human, he's a rubber man."

Before he left the Olympic Village, Michael paid Coach Knight a compliment. But when he was asked if he would have liked to play his college ball under Knight's dictatorial and abusive style of coaching, Michael just smiled and said, "I'd have to think about that."

Up until that point in his life Michael had always been part of a strong program with a winning tradition. From the triumphant ways of UNC to the glory days at the Olympics, Michael had only tasted success. But now he was headed for Chicago; he was headed down. Far from being champions, the Bulls hadn't even made the playoffs in the preceding three years (in a league where more teams make the playoffs than don't). And as far as winning traditions were concerned, there were none. The Bulls had managed to play better than .500 ball only twice in the preceding nine seasons. Would Michael be sucked into that quicksand of mediocrity, or would he be able to use his special skills and desire to transform the Bulls into a contender?

13

3

Dazzled

Michael was coming into a situation in Chicago that placed a heavy burden on his 21-year-old shoulders. The Bulls had finished the preceding season with the second-worst record in the entire league. He was flying into the Windy City carrying a lot of expectations with him. He was being viewed by many Chicagoans as a savior—the Moses who would lead the Bulls out of the desert and into the Promised Land of the playoffs. And the owners of the Bulls were also counting on Michael to bring fans into Chicago Stadium.

The fans in Chicago were hungry for a winner, and their appetites were being fed a constant banquet of Michael Jordan hype by the media.

Everywhere that the Bulls played, they were followed by a flock of television cameras, radio and print reporters, and thousands of excited fans. Michael was followed and mobbed as if he were a rock star. And what made these scenes even more unusual for a basketball team was the fact that it was going on in the preseason! Michael, surprised at all the attention, just smiled and noted, "I mean, I haven't even played a regular-season game yet."

Even before his first pro game, though, it was obvious that Michael possessed a special quality that made him more than just another basketball star, a quality that transcended the game of basketball. The media and the fans were reacting not only to Michael's awesome acrobatic ability but also to the handsome, easy-to-smile, well-spoken, and thoughtful person that he is.

ProServ, a company that represents some athletes in their business affairs, saw early on that Michael's rare combination of attributes would make him an ideal spokesperson for companies. An executive at ProServ, David Falk, and Nike were so assured of Michael's appeal that they worked out a unique deal. Nike agreed to bring out a special line of sneakers and other sports

14

apparel with Michael's own logo on it. The deal, which gave Michael a royalty on every Air Jordan article that Nike sold, almost instantly turned into a multi-million-dollar bonanza for Michael and for Nike. Air Jordan had taken off!

David Falk was quickly besieged by offers from a host of companies that wanted Michael to represent them. But Michael and David were only interested in having Michael associated with companies and products that he felt comfortable endorsing or representing. Eventually, lucrative agreements that pay Michael millions of dollars a year were worked out with, in addition to Nike, McDonalds, Coca-Cola, Wilson Sporting Goods, Chevrolet, and Guy LaRouche watches.

In the meantime, though, it was show time, time for Michael to begin earning the five-year, four-million-dollar contract that had made him the highest-paid rookie guard in the history of the NBA.

Michael got out of the chute quickly. He scored 25 points or more in ten of his first fifteen games as a pro, including a 37-point bombing of the Milwaukee Bucks and a 45-point rampage against the San Antonio Spurs.

But Michael didn't really feel into the flow of the NBA. He knew that he had limitations: His outside shot needed work, and he didn't drive to his left side as well as he did to his right. He knew that he had to improve his jump shot and his moves to the left so that defenses couldn't sag, waiting for the drive, and overplay him to the right. A lot of other players would have been content, even thrilled, to explode on the scene as Michael had. But Michael knew he had to work on those weaknesses if he wanted to take his game to another level; and he did work, every day in practice.

While Michael was working on his game, he was continuing to waste NBA defenses. In one memorable sequence he single-handedly brought the Bulls back to defeat the Los Angeles Clippers. First he popped an 18-foot jump shot to tie the game with 1:26 left. Then, playing tough defense, he forced Norm Nixon into throwing up an air ball. Calwell Jones picked off the shot and threw an outlet pass that Michael chased down near midcourt. Michael dribbled toward the basket, but while he was in the air, all set to dunk, Derek Smith wrapped him in a midair bear hug. As the players were falling toward the floor, Michael tossed the ball up, and yes, it went in. The Los Angeles crowd, momentarily stunned into silence, quickly rose to its feet and burst into applause as some fans chanted "USA! USA!" as a salute to Michael's shot and his feats in the Olympic games. Even Derek Smith was amazed. "It was incredible. Most people wouldn't have even gotten the ball out of their hands."

As Michael flew around the league performing his aerial acrobatics, he continued to draw raves and set new standards. Hubie Brown, who was the coach of the New York Knicks and not a man given to easy praise, paid the rookie the ultimate compliment by comparing him to Larry Bird. "The young man is blessed with so much natural talent, and then he plays at such a fever pitch. Jordan is always—or most nights—playing or performing on all cylinders at the top of his potential. He's a lot like Bird. They are special." Brown, a demanding coach, was as impressed with Michael's intensity and work habits as he was with his natural talent.

Then, in a game against Bird and the Celtics, Michael turned it up another notch as he poured in 41 points, dished out seven assists, and hauled down 12 rebounds. Larry Bird had now seen him live and close up, and even he was dazzled. "Never seen anyone like him. He's the best ever. Yep, at this stage, he's doing more than I ever did. I couldn't do what he does as a rookie. Heck, there was one drive tonight, he had the ball in his right hand, then he took it down, then he brought it back up. I got a hand on it, fouled him, and he still scored. You have to play the game to realize how difficult that is. You see that and figure, 'Well, what the heck can you do?' "

One of the few sour notes that Michael experienced during his first season occurred at the All-Star game. Voted on to the starting team, Michael was able to score only seven points in 22 minutes of play, largely because he didn't get to touch the ball very often. Michael and others believe that it was a plan by Magic Johnson and Isaiah Thomas to "freeze the rookie out and teach him a lesson." Two days later, in a game against Isaiah and the Detroit Pistons, Michael played the teacher as he pumped and dunked for 49 points.

By the end of the season Michael could have qualified as a full professor. He finished third in the league in scoring with a 28.2 average and first in total points scored, 2,313. Michael also led the Bulls in steals with 196, or 2.4 per game (fourth best in the league); assists, with 5.9 per game; and rebounds, with 6.5 per game. He became only the third player in NBA history to lead a team in points, steals, assists, and rebounds in a single season. (Dave Cowens, who played center for the Celtics, and Larry Bird are the other two.) He capped off his spectacular season by being selected as the Schick Pivotal Player of the Year and the NBA's Rookie of the Year.

Michael's phenomenal performance led the Bulls to a 38–44 record—not championship caliber, but a big improvement over the previous year and good enough to get them into the playoffs. The Bulls, though, didn't have enough depth or overall talent to match up with the better teams in the intensified atmosphere of the playoffs, and they were bounced by the Bucks, three games to one, despite the fact that Michael ripped the cords for a 29.3 scoring average in the series.

Michael was disappointed at the early departure of the Bulls from the playoffs, but he was able to look back at his rookie season with a tremendous sense of accomplishment and some relief, too. "I really didn't know how good I could be [in the pros]. Everyone on the coaching staff at UNC was telling me that I'd do fine, but you really don't know. I went in with a clear head, just to go out and try to contribute and do the best I could. I know expectations were way above my head. I never thought I could reach them; but I surprised myself, and I surprised a lot of them." Michael didn't just surprise; he dazzled!

Although Michael had been concerned about trying to carve out a place for himself in the highly competitive NBA, a workplace that is so demanding that only a few hundred human beings are good enough to work in it, he still found the time to care for others. One time, for example, after playing a tough game and getting only five hours of sleep, he went to film a commercial for the Special Olympics. During the day Michael worked with children suffering from Down's syndrome, and one girl especially became attached to Michael. He talked with her and helped her make a layup, and she paid him back with a hug. When Michael began to leave, the girl began to cry. Michael, feeling her hurt, walked back and hugged her until her sobs stopped.

Michael doesn't make a lot of noise about lending a hand or making a financial contribution, and he doesn't pat himself on the back about it either. "Basketball, all my fans—they have given a lot to me. This is my way of giving something back to the community. I'll always remember when I wasn't so popular."

It had been an important year for Michael. He had realized his dream of playing in the NBA and discovered that he didn't merely belong but that he could dominate. He had signed contracts in and out of basketball that made him financially secure for the rest of his life. And most important of all, he had grown as a person. He was no longer the shy little boy but a man who was at peace with himself.

4

A Dark Cloud

Michael began his second season in the NBA with a lot of optimism. He was more confident of his abilities, and he and his teammates were more accustomed to playing with each other. Michael's rosy outlook seemed well placed as the Bulls began the 1984–85 season by jumping out to a 3–0 record.

But dark clouds appear even where eagles soar; and in the fourth game most of Michael's season was washed away when he came crashing down and fractured a bone in his left foot.

Michael spent the first few weeks after the injury on the Bulls' bench, watching them play and—mostly—lose. "My body could stand the crutches, but my mind couldn't stand the sidelines." So Michael packed his bags and headed back to Chapel Hill and the classroom. While Michael was hitting the books at UNC, the fans around the league showed that he wasn't forgotten by making him the top vote-getter for the East squad in the All-Star game, despite the fact that he wouldn't be able to play.

When Michael felt that his foot had healed sufficiently, he began testing its strength while playing himself back into shape in local pickup games. The Bulls' management was edgy. They didn't want Michael to play too soon and risk further injury or permanent damage. But Michael has a special article in his contract, a "love of the game" clause, that allows him to play in pickup games just about whenever he wants to.

With a few weeks left in the season Michael announced that he was ready to return to the Bulls. Jerry Krause, Chicago's general manager, wanted Michael to sit out the remainder of the season. He didn't want Michael's career put at risk, and he might also have thought that if the Bulls kept losing the way they were, they would get a high pick in the upcoming college draft. Maybe they could select a player good enough to make them a serious contender for years to come.

Michael certainly wanted to play on a stronger team, and he was going to get paid whether he played or not. But there's a fire that burns in Michael, and he wasn't about to let the desire be doused by trading the present for the future. "The doctors said there was a ten-percent chance I'd reinjure it. I figured ninety percent was pretty good odds. I knew I had the desire and the urge. When management didn't want to recognize that, it was the one time I felt treated like a piece of meat."

While Michael was away, the Bulls went into a tailspin, dropping 43 games and winning only 19. With Michael back and leading the way, they picked up the pace enough to just sneak into the playoffs with a 30–52 record.

That was the good news; the bad news was that their opponent in the best-of-five series was the Boston Celtics, the team that would go on to capture the NBA championship.

Michael played magnificently in the opening game of the series, but his 49 points couldn't overcome the combined talents of a great Boston team playing on their home court, and the Bulls went down, 123–104.

In the second game, also played on the fabled parquet floor of the ancient Boston Garden, Michael was simply in another zone. Watching him going up and over defenders, twisting and spinning to defeat double- and triple-teaming, soaring into the air above flailing arms, and then slamming the ball through the basket, it seemed that Michael was unstoppable. In an awesome display of individual brilliance, Michael poured in 63 points to break the all-time playoff scoring record. And still it wasn't enough. The Celtics answered every shot and held on to win in double overtime, 135–131.

The teams had played full-out, playoff basketball from the opening tip-off until the final buzzer, but the game, as thrilling as it was, was overshadowed by Michael's magnificent performance. Even the players were awed by Michael's artistry. Dennis Johnson, considered to be one of the best defensive players of all time, admitted, "I wasn't guarding him. No one was guarding him. No one *can* guard him." Larry Bird expressed his feelings quickly: "Maybe the guy is God disguised as Michael Jordan."

Michael's 63-point effort eclipsed a record that had been

established by the great Elgin Baylor in 1962. It was fitting that Michael should break Baylor's record, because there is a thread that connects the two of them. Baylor was the founding member of a very exclusive three-man club—the three players who have seemed able to defy the laws of gravity and walk on air. "I've heard that Elgin Baylor could do great things," says Michael, speaking about the ex-Laker. "And there is Dr. J [Julius Erving], who could soar, but I didn't see him at his best. But I guess he took it to another level from Elgin, and maybe I've taken it to another level after that."

In the third game the Celtics held Michael to 18 points and romped over the Bulls, 122–104. While the Bulls couldn't avoid being swept out of the playoffs, Michael did break the record for total points scored in a three-game series, with 131. The previous record was set in 1960 by the great center Wilt Chamberlain, who had scored 116 points.

Michael was grateful that he hadn't reinjured his foot and pleased by his record-setting performances. But basketball is a team game, and Michael, for all his individual brilliance, is a team player. So the individual scoring records didn't ease the pain of the early elimination from the playoffs for the second consecutive year.

5

Taking It to Another Level

Before the 1986–87 season began, Michael earned his Bachelor of Arts degree in geography from UNC, and the Bulls signed up a new coach, Doug Collins. Once the season began, it was like one long Michael Jordan highlight film. Someone once gave Dominique Wilkins, the exciting forward of the Atlanta Hawks, the nickname "The Human Highlights Film," but as Danny Ainge, Boston's All-Star guard, observed, "If you had to choose one highlights film to watch, it would be Michael Jordan's."

He began the season by burning the Knicks for 50 points and he stayed on fire until the season was finished. In his first trip back to Boston since the 63-point game, he nicked the nets for Chicago's first 19 points, on his way to 49. Against the Knicks again, he bagged the Bulls' final 18 points, including the game-winning bucket with only seconds left on the clock. Game after game, in every city in the league, Michael worked his magic and brought the crowds to their feet.

When the league totaled up the fans' vote for the All-Star game, Michael was the top vote-getter. The day before the game the best jammers in the league go up against each other in a slam-dunk contest, in which points are awarded for original-ity, degree of difficulty, and making the shot. In the contest Michael put on an electrifying exhibition of dribbling, jumping, and stuffing that left the competition shaking their heads.

Michael brought the crowd at the Kingdome in Seattle out of their seats with his "kiss the rim" dunk. He took the ball at half court and dribbled to the left baseline; then he launched himself and, while moving through the air toward the basket, passed the ball through his legs. Then, stretched out parallel to the ground, still floating toward the basket, he ducked his head under the rim, seeming to brush it with his lips, and on the other side of the hoop sent a thunderous windmill slam dunk, like a bolt from

Zeus down through the net. The fans at the Kingdome roared, and the other competitors marveled. "It was fantastic," exclaimed Terence Stansbury. "It was even better on replay because you couldn't see it all the first time around."

Almost before the audience had a chance to catch its breath, Michael was at it again, performing the routine that clinched the contest. He started out under the basket and dribbled down to the far foul line. When he hit the line, his tongue wagging, he launched himself toward the basket. He appeared to level off for an instant, but then the afterburners kicked in and Michael, seeming to fly, rose up above the basket and slammed the ball down through the net. The crowd in the Kingdome went wild, and all across the country fans in front of their television sets rubbed their eyes in disbelief at the Michael Jordan flying machine.

Even Michael was impressed. "When I look back on that dunking contest, it's just unbelievable that I was able to do those things." When his Bulls' teammates look back on the contest, though, they remember that Michael took the $12,500 prize money and gave each of the eleven $1,000. "I did it because my teammates had been so understanding. There was a lack of animosity over all the attention I get, and they had all been caring. They had worked so hard, and I got all the publicity and credit. Those guys deserved something. I've seen stars isolate themselves. Not me. I like to go to meals with the guys and pick up the tab, like a quarterback with his linemen," said Michael, stealing a page from ex-Chicago Bears' quarterback Jim McMahon's notebook.

Bulls' Coach Doug Collins provides some insight as to why the other players bang the boards and get Michael the ball when he gets to take about a third of all the shots. "The other guys wouldn't work so hard for him if he wasn't such a terrific guy. His example alone makes the other guys better and my job easier."

Michael had quietly added another segment to his highlights film early in the new year. But this one didn't happen on the court, and no one videotaped it. Michael became engaged to Ms. Juanita Vanoy, a Chicago businesswoman.

After the All-Star break Michael continued his scoring splurge through the cities of the NBA. In one memorable stretch he went nine straight games in which he scored 40 or more points, making a serious run at Wilt Chamberlain's record of 14-straight, which Wilt accomplished twice.

Michael's high-octane performances seemed to serve as motivation for other sharpshooters around the league, all of whom wanted to hold their own against Michael's onslaught—especially on their home courts. "I guess I make guys feel I'm invading their turf," observed Michael after Dominique Wilkins had battered the Bulls with a 57-point effort. "It's the old playground code," smiled Michael, "and it adds to the fun." Michael also realized that even fans in the other cities came to see him perform his aerial artistry. "What the fans on the road want to see is me get fifty and their team win."

Michael didn't have too much fun, though, when Dominique and the Hawks came into Chicago for an April game. The Bulls lost 117–114 despite an amazing performance by Michael, in which he set an NBA record by scoring 23 consecutive points for the Bulls on his way to a sensational 61-point night. That point production put Michael over the 3,000 mark and made him only the second player in NBA history to score that many points in a single season. Wilt Chamberlain was the first. After the game, though, Michael was depressed rather than delighted. "I know that I am the only guard in the history of basketball to have scored this many points. But the records mean nothing. I'd rather have had the win because it would have clinched the seventh playoff spot in the Eastern conference."

The Bulls finally did make the playoffs despite their unimpressive 40–42 record. But their presence was short-lived, as Boston beat them three straight again, despite Michael's 35.7 average.

Michael was disappointed at Chicago's early departure from the playoffs. He had worked so hard all season long, in games and in practice, where Michael also goes at full throttle. As Doug Collins notes, "He's easily the best practice player I've ever seen." Some people, in fact, think that Michael should slow down a little in practice and coast when a game is in the bag or out of reach. But Michael's engine only runs in one gear—overdrive. "I never pace myself. I know a lot of people think I'll wear myself down. Someday maybe I will burn out physically.

24

But the desire will always burn. I'll always go full speed until I give out."

Michael's desire and unmatched talent has turned him into the most potent player in basketball, and his astonishing aeronautical artistry make him the most popular drawing card in the NBA. (The Bulls set a home attendance record and were second to the Celtics in road attendance.)

The mediocre record and early playoff elimination of the Bulls didn't detract from the magnificence of Michael's season. He had begun the season with the 50-pointer against the Knicks, and he didn't let up until he finished his fabulous season with the fifth-highest average (37.1) in the history of the NBA. (Wilt Chamberlain owns the top four spots.) Michael matched two of Chamberlain's records by scoring 60 or more points twice in a season and 50 or more in three consecutive games. He scored 50 or more eight times and 40 or more 37 times. And he scored 30 or more in all but 15 of the Bulls' 82-game schedule! In addition to his sensational season-long scoring spree, Michael became the first player in the history of the league to record more than 200 steals (he had 236) and 100 blocked shots in one season. His total of 125 blocks in a single season was the most ever by a guard. Michael was also named All-NBA First Team after being named Player of the Month twice during the season, and he was the runner-up to Magic Johnson in the MVP voting.

Michael appreciated his awards, but he was annoyed that his defensive skills weren't recognized by the voters. "I'd rather make All-Defense than All-NBA." It isn't that Michael needed another award or had an ego problem. It's only that he felt the judges completely overlooked the results he had produced. "Michael Cooper [who had not only made the team but was chosen as Defensive Player of the Year] is great at ball denial," Michael noted. "But check his other stats [only 78 steals and 43 blocked shots]. This league gives defensive awards on reputation. It just tees me off."

Jerry Reynolds, an assistant coach and an astute observer, put Michael's magnificent season and talent in its true perspective. "The thing is, every time you see him, he does something different. You might see a Dominique or a Clyde Drexler and think they're just as good. Then you see Jordan again and say, 'No way!' The other guys put on a great show, but Michael takes it to another level. And when he can concentrate on it, he's a totally great defensive player, as good as there is in the league.

"As an opponent you just try to contain him. If Jordan gets forty, okay, you can hold the rest of the team to sixty-five. But you're really afraid he's just going to go nuts. Jordan's the only player in the league you can say that about."

6

The Amazing Flying Machine

Before the 1987–88 season began, Michael was stung by criticism that the Bulls played like a one-man team—Team Jordan—and that Michael was a one-dimensional player. Larry Bird, for one, said, "I don't like to watch the same guy take every shot. That's not what the game is about."

It might be argued that the game is about winning and that a team's best shot is to do what it does best and to do it as often as it can. And while it's true that Michael averages about thirty percent of the Bulls' shots, it's also true that he scores even more than thirty percent of their points.

It should also be pointed out that Michael is also always up among the team leaders in rebounds, assists, blocked shots, and steals. And Larry Bird might recall that he had similar shooting statistics when he was forced to carry the scoring load on his college team. Not everyone is fortunate enough to play with talent-rich teams like the Celtics, Lakers, or Pistons. The fact is that the Bulls haven't provided Michael with a strong supporting cast with whom to share the load. The other general managers in the league don't burn up Jerry Krause's telephone wires trying to trade for any of the other Bulls, with the exception of strong forward Charles Oakley (who now wears a New York Knicks uniform).

But instead of sulking when he heard the criticism, Michael used it as a positive motivating tool. "I'm taking these raps as a challenge to get better."

If there was one thing that the other coaches and players in the league didn't need or want to deal with, it was a better, souped-up version of Michael Jordan, the Amazing Flying Machine.

Coaches were already spending sleepless nights trying to devise defenses to contain Michael—not to stop him, mind you, just to limit the damage. No one thinks that Michael can be shut down. "We figure he's going to get his forty points," explained Denver's Doug Moe. "We just try to make him work hard and take a lot of shots to get there."

Some coaches set up their defenses to try to push Michael toward the baseline, where he has less room to operate. But that's fine with Michael. "I've always had a lot of success there. Somehow I'm able to avoid the contact better there . . . and there are fewer defenders."

Other teams try to force him to the middle, where there are usually more players, more arms and legs, for Michael to maneuver through. But Sidney Moncreif, a many-time member of the NBA's All-Defensive team, knows the pitfalls in using that strategy against the man he calls "the most talented offensive player in basketball." He says, "Generally, there will be more passing options, more ways for him to break your defense down, in the middle."

Ultimately Michael reduces all plans to stop him to fading chalk on coaches' blackboards, because so much of what he does is improvisational. As Alvin Robertson, the great defensive guard of the San Antonio Spurs, points out, "The things that Michael does are so exciting and creative that he'll get the crowd behind him, and even the guys on the *other team's* bench will be sitting there saying, 'Did you see that?'"

Watching Michael create may be the prettiest sight in sports. As he goes into the air, a cross between a gold-medal gymnastics champion and a world-class ballet dancer, he lifts athletics into the realm of the artistic. When he takes off toward the basket, Michael seems to hover like a helicopter, scanning the court, waiting for his defenders to be brought back to the floor by the force of gravity while he hangs, stretches, and then slams the ball down through the hoop—*swish*!

"I never practice the fancy stuff," says Michael. "If I thought about a move, I'd probably turn the ball over. I just look at a situation in the air, adjust, create, and let instinct take over."

When Michael is asked how he would tell someone to guard him, he answers, "It's the same with me as with any strong offensive player. The outside shot is definitely the weaker aspect, the lesser of two evils. If you can get him to miss the first couple of shots from outside, maybe it will affect him mentally. Of course," Michael warns with a smile, "if he hits his first few and gets his confidence going, that may be the night he scores fifty." Michael explains that his game is as much mental as it is physical. It takes him one game to figure out what will work best against the defender. "When I get up in the air, everything is instinctive, but the rest of the time, all the other things I do, I'm thinking."

Michael Cooper, the swing man for the LA Lakers, laughs when people talk about defensing Michael. "When people say I, or anyone else, do a good job on Michael, that's wrong. There's *no way* I stop him. I need the whole team. As soon as he touches the ball, he electrifies the intensity inside you. The alarm goes off because you don't know *what* he's going to do. He goes right, left, over you, around you. He twists, he turns, and you *know* he's going to get his shot off. You just don't know how and when. That's the most devastating thing, psychologically, to a defender."

Michael and the Bulls sailed through the first half of the regular season in super shape, with just a brief pause for Michael to defend his slam-dunk crown and compete in the All-Star game. Michael just nipped Dominique Wilkins in the finals of the slam-dunk when he scored a perfect 50 on his final attempt. Afterward Michael graciously acknowledged that the judges might have been influenced by the screaming, sold-out crowd in Chicago Stadium. "If it hadn't been in Chicago, it might have gone the other way."

The next day, though, in the All-Star game, it went only one way—the Jordan Express-way. Before the game Boston's Kevin McHale told Michael, "You've seemed tentative in other All-Star games. Just pretend you're playing a game for the Bulls." Michael took the advice and put on a dazzling display for the home town crowd. With just under seven minutes left in the game, Michael, who had popped and slammed for 24 points, was sitting on the bench with four fouls. When the West team started to cut into the East team's lead, the 18,403 fans in Chicago Stadium began to chant, "We want Michael, we want Michael."

Two minutes later Michael was back in the game. And a few minutes after that Michael had pumped in 16 more points in the final minutes to finish with 40, and led the East team to a 138–133 victory.

When Michael had reached 36 points, Isaiah Thomas told him that he and Larry Bird were going to help him get 40. "I didn't think anyone had ever scored forty in an All-Star game," Thomas said. Isaiah did his part as he first set Michael up for a seventeen-foot jumper for one bucket and then arched him a perfect alley-oop lob that Michael dunked for his fortieth point. With just a few seconds left, Thomas and Bird were still trying. Isaiah signaled for an isolation play for Michael. Bird got the ball, unaware that Michael was only two points away from tying Chamberlain's All-Star game scoring record. "But the crowd was screaming and I sensed something." Bird threw a perfect lead pass to Michael, but he just pulled up short and with a big smile shook his head "no" and let the ball sail out of bounds. "I felt a little embarrassed at the end. I didn't want to steal the show from the game itself. I'd had a great game and thought all my points up to thirty-six were earned. I thought the guys were really going out of their way to get me the ball on the last two baskets, and at this point I didn't think we needed any more points. And I didn't want anything handed to me."

When Michael was presented with the MVP award, he thanked his teammates and the fans. "This was," he smiled, "a picture-perfect weekend."

Michael and the Bulls closed the regular schedule with a rush. In the last week of the season Michael wasted the Knicks with a 47-point performance. Rick Pitino, New York's rookie coach, just shook his head and quipped, "He was like Superman, and I didn't have any kryptonite."

The Bulls finished with their best record since Michael's arrival, 50–32, and in second place in the tough Central Division.

They opened the playoffs at home against the young and talented Cleveland Cavaliers, determined to make it past the first round. Michael took matters into his own hands by unleashing an avalanche of points in the first two games, 50 in a 104–93 victory and then 55 in a 106–101 win. Michael not only scored half of his team's total points in the two games, but he also became the first player in history to bag back-to-back 50-pointers in the playoffs. Wayne Embry, the general manager of the Cavs and a former All-Star center in the NBA, acknowledged Michael's mastery. "He plays higher than anybody's ever played. He plays so high that even the big guys can't challenge him."

In the next two games Michael, playing with a sore back and an aching right knee, which he had injured in game one, scored "only" 38 and 44 points, and the Cavs, playing at home, gored the Bulls twice to even the series at two games apiece.

With the Bulls' season hanging in the balance in the fifth and final game, Michael came through with a 39-point performance, leading a balanced Bulls attack that toppled Cleveland 107–101. Michael's 226 total points were the most ever scored in a five-game series, but more importantly the Bulls had finally escaped early elimination.

The joy was short-lived, though, because their second-round opponents were the tough, talented Detroit Pistons. And the team from the Motor City was on a mission to avenge its own heartbreaking loss to the Celtics in the 1987 Eastern finals. The Pistons just steamrolled right over the flat Bulls. They blanketed Michael with two and three defenders, and none of his team-mates were able to rise to the occasion and relieve the pressure. Depressed, Michael was left to lament, "It's difficult to beat a defense by yourself."

While Michael was disappointed at not going further in the playoffs, his season in every other way was an unqualified success. He had won his second-straight scoring title with a 35.0 average. He had registered more than 200 steals (totaling a league-leading 259) and blocked more than 100 shots (131), the second consecutive year that he had done what no other player had *ever* done. This year, though, the judges recognized his achievements, and he was named Defensive Player of the Year. Michael was also selected as the NBA's Most Valuable Player and became the only player to ever win the MVP award, the Defensive Player of the Year award, and the scoring title in one season. It was an absolutely astonishing achievement.

At this point in his career Michael is already considered by many to be the best player in the game, maybe the best of all time. As Magic Johnson said, "Everybody always says it's me and Larry [Bird]. Really it's Mike and everybody else."

He has won all the individual awards and is still getting better. But Michael would trade all his trophies for one championship ring. Watching Michael up in the air, creating, is the most exciting sight in sports; seeing Michael play with a championship-caliber team would be an even bigger treat.

7

Off the Court

Michael lives in a suburban townhouse in Northbrook, Illinois. He does a lot of his own cooking and cleaning because he doesn't believe in hiring maids or "servants." He still likes to relax by shooting pool, bowling, and playing golf. Golf, in fact, has become a passion for Michael, just as it has for fellow Chicagoan and ex-Bears' quarterback Jim McMahon. Michael always tries to play at least 18 holes a day and has been known to play as many as 54. He even talks of becoming a professional golfer after he hangs up his Air Jordans and retires. But fortunately for basketball fans, that time is a long time away. "I've got the greatest job in America," says Michael. "Could anything be better than being paid a lot of money to do what you love most?"

Michael also spends a lot of his time on his many business ventures. His deals are so numerous that he employs nearly a dozen people to assist him with his business affairs. In addition to his representation of Nike ("I love them right out of the box," he says. "No blisters or anything."), Coke, McDonalds, and the others, Michael also set up JUMP (Jordan Universal Marketing Promotions). His parents act as vice-presidents of JUMP and also operate Michael's auto-parts store and Nike sportswear outlet back home in North Carolina.

"It took getting used to," says Michael, "but now I enjoy all the off-court stuff. It's like being back in school. I'm learning all the time. In college I never realized the opportunities available to a pro athlete. I've been given the chance to meet all kinds of people, to travel and expand my financial capabilities, to get ideas and learn about life, to create a world apart from basketball."

Although Michael has achieved stunning success and lifetime financial security (it is estimated that he earns well over five million dollars per year, with more than half coming from sources other than his basketball contract), he hasn't become full of himself. As teammate John Paxson noted, "Being the dominating force on a team hasn't given Michael an ego problem. He could be real arrogant and let the press go to his head, but he never does. He cares about his teammates as people."

Michael, the super athlete, successful businessman, and world traveler, has remained true to himself and the values that he grew up with. And he still remembers the ninth-grader who couldn't dunk or even jump high. He remembers the work, the practices. "I'm not caught up in the flashy life. I haven't changed my personality at all. I know where I came from and what it took to get me where I am. I still love kids and working with kids."

Michael doesn't just talk about his feelings for children; he spends time visiting them in hospitals and bringing smiles to their faces and laughter into their lives. Their eyes show that Michael is someone special, not because he's a great basketball player but because the children feel that he really cares.

Michael was once selected as a finalist, along with Darryl Strawberry and Jim McMahon, in a nationwide poll of youngsters under the age of seventeen for the Outstanding Male Athlete of the Year. Michael beamed when he heard the news. "I think this award is going to be more treasured than any other award I have, because it's the admiration of young kids, my peers actually, and I'm very thankful."

Michael, with all of his commitments, always finds the time to sign autographs, read as much of his fan mail as he can, and make sure that all of it gets answered along with requests for autographed pictures. And when kids tell Michael that they want to be just like him, he thanks them and says, "The first lesson: Don't be like me. Be better than me. That's the goal."

And when Michael leaves Chicago Stadium after a tough game, he still takes the time to talk to the vendors and the maintenance men before he heads home.

There is no doubt that Michael is a superstar, but more importantly, he is a super person.

8

The Greatest

Michael appreciated the individual awards and the acknowledgment by most observers that he was the greatest talent in the game. But what Michael really hungered for was a strong supporting cast that would allow the Bulls to take a serious run at an NBA championship.

Michael didn't want to become the basketball equivalent of another great Chicago athlete, Ernie Banks. Banks, who played for the Cubs for 19 years starting in 1953, twice led the NL in home runs and also won two MVP awards. He was so good and so popular that he became known as Mr. Cub, but he's also known as the best baseball player who never played in a World Series.

The Bulls did make an offseason trade with the Knicks for Bill Cartright in an attempt to fill their long-standing void at center. But the seven-foot Cartright didn't fit the bill. Instead of moving up in the Central Division standings, the Bulls were sinking toward the bottom.

As the 1988–89 season headed into the homestretch, Michael —surprise, surprise—was leading the NBA in scoring and in steals. But he was also leading the league in minutes played, trying to plug all the holes in the Bulls' lineup by himself. Michael tried to downplay his efforts: "Hey, I'm a young thoroughbred, and thoroughbreds don't need rest." But thoroughbreds usually don't have to pull wagons up a hill, and given Chicago's lack of team talent, it was as though Michael was trying to pull a very heavy wagon up a very steep hill.

In order to cut down on the wear and tear on Michael's body and because the Bulls didn't have an effective point guard, Doug Collins decided to move Michael from shooting guard to the point. "I felt like we were struggling to get the ball to Michael. I felt the only way we were going to fix that was to get the ball into

Michael's hands in the backcourt, let him push the ball and dictate the tempo of the game."

Although the move came in March, with more than half the season gone and no time to really practice, Michael picked up on his new role as if he had been playing the point his entire career. In his first 17 games at the point position, Michael bagged nine triple-doubles, including five in a row. (By comparison, Magic Johnson, who has played at point guard since high school, led the league with 17 triple-doubles.)

Despite having to sacrifice his own point totals for the final 24 games of the season, Michael still managed to capture his third consecutive scoring title. And he also recorded personal bests in field-goal percentage, free-throw percentage, rebounds, and assists.

But Michael's herculean efforts weren't enough to stop the Bulls from closing the season with a loud thud. They lost nine of their last 11 games and slipped down to a fifth-place finish in the Central Division. And their immediate prospects didn't appear to be any brighter, because they drew the Cleveland Cavaliers, the team that had tied the Lakers for the second-best record in the NBA, as their opponent in the opening round of the play-offs. The Cavs had beaten the Bulls six straight times during the season, and even the hometown Chicago sportscasters were predicting that the Cavs would sweep the Bulls right out of the play-offs.

Michael realized that he had to do something to rally the spirit of his team, so he publicly predicted that the Bulls would win the best-of-five series in four games. "I wanted to motivate the team. I wanted to get them to accept the challenge. I knew that I was motivated. I just wanted to make sure they were."

Michael showed just how ready he was by leading the Bulls to an upset win on the Cavs home court in game one. During a third-quarter time-out Michael walked over to the press table and razzed the Chicago reporters about their prediction: "Sweep, my butt!"

The Bulls dropped the second game as Michael played out of control and committed seven turnovers. After the game Michael disregarded the 30 points he had poured in. "I was horsespit. I was overmotivated. I tried to force things. But we realize now that we can beat this ballclub."

The teams traveled to Chicago, where they split the next two games. Michael jammed for 44 points to lead the Bulls to a win in game three, but the Cavs evened the series with a 108–105 over-time win in game four. After the game Michael was really down. He had soared over and run through the helpless Cav defenders on his way to a 50-point outburst, but he had also missed a free throw with only nine seconds left that could have tied the game. Michael wasn't interested in his point production or in pointing the finger at any of his teammates. "I can't pin it on anybody but me. All the missed opportunities from that point were my fault."

Air Jordan was grounded, but only for as long as it took to tip-off for the decisive fifth game. In the first half Michael played like a classic point guard, trying to get everyone involved in the of-fense. But in the second half, with the season on the line, Michael poured 30 points through the nets, including 11 in the last two minutes and four in the final six seconds. And it was the final .06 that showed Michael's incomparable.

With the Bulls trailing by a point, Michael hit a jump shot over Jim Nance to give them a 99–98 lead. After Craig Ehlo hit a driving layup to reclaim the lead for the Cavs, the Bulls called a time-out with three ticks left in their season.

Doug Collins diagrammed a play on the sideline blackboard, but everyone in the building knew who the ball was going to. There was no second option. As the Bulls broke the huddle, Michael told Craig Hodges, "Don't worry. I'm going to hit this sucker."

And then Michael juked around two defenders; took the in-bound toss; dribbled twice; pulled up a few feet behind the free-throw line; and as time expired, and with Ehlo's outstretched hand in his face, put up a jump shot that whispered s-w-i-s-h as it sliced through the net.

Everybody in the arena was startled, but no one was surprised. And Michael was in orbit. "This is probably the biggest shot I've made in the NBA. I was crushed after I missed that free throw in game four. A lot of people think that can't happen to a person who has achieved as much as I have. But I made a prediction to get everybody pumped up so we wouldn't get swept. I put my butt on the block and I missed a chance to lock it up. Then I came here and got booed in the introductions. I heard them tell me it was time to set up my tee times for the summer. I felt I had something to prove."

That Michael could still feel that he had anything left to prove indicates how brightly the competitive fire burns within him and propels him to new heights, new achievements. Despite all the scoring titles, the awards and the accolades, despite the $25 million contract, Michael will never feel as if he's arrived. There will always be some new challenge out in front of him. Michael's next challenge was the New York Knicks, fresh from a three-game sweep of Charles Barkley and the 76ers. Although the Knicks were favored to win, Michael refused to be intimidated by the underdog role that had again been assigned to the Bulls. "I hope that everyone picks the Knicks to sweep, because we'll just use that as energy."

All by himself Michael put out enough energy in game one to light up Madison Square Garden. And when the two teams went into overtime, Michael kicked into overdrive, outscoring the entire Knicks team in the extra period to give the Bulls a 120–109 win.

The Knicks did manage to pull the plug on Michael in game two. Using constant double teaming and a trapping defense, they held Michael to 15 points, his all-time lowest production in a play-off game. But Michael bounced back in a big way in the next two games, electrifying the fans and giving the Bulls a commanding three-games-to-one lead.

It seemed that Michael was everywhere, controling everything. He doubled down low on defense to deny the ball to Patrick Ewing, the Knicks' main offensive threat. And on offense he constantly beat the Knicks vaunted press to create easy baskets at the other end. His presence on the court was so dominating that he seemed to singlehandedly stifle the Knicks and spark the Bulls. Rick Pitino, the Knicks' coach, was quick to acknowledge Michael's artistry. "When Michael first came into the league, everybody questioned whether he made his teammates better. But right now, if you had to say who the best player is, you'd say Michael Jordan. Not only is he great, but he is raising the play of everyone on his team."

The New Yorkers hung in to win the fifth game, despite a 38-point spree by Michael, but that was their last gasp. The Knicks did battle the Bulls down to the wire in the sixth game, but every time they came close, Michael canned a pair of free throws. The Knicks tied the game for the last time with six seconds left when guard Trent Tucker bagged a rare four-point play.

The Bulls called time-out, and both coaches discussed strategy, but it didn't take a rocket scientist to figure out who the ball was going to in this situation. Michael defeated the double team on the inbound play, drove the lane, and drew the foul with .04 showing on the clock. Then he calmly went to the free throw line and sank the two free throws that sunk the Knicks season. "We wanted to deny Jordan the ball," explained a frustrated Rick Pitino. "But hey, he's the best player to ever put on a uniform. He did it to Cleveland and now he's done it to us."

Michael had carried the Bulls farther than anyone else had expected, and now they were only four wins away from the championship round. But blocking their way were the Detroit Pistons. The Bad Boys from the Motor City, known for playing the best and most bruising defense in the NBA. But Michael served notice that he wasn't going to be intimidated, by leading the Bulls to a big win in the first game. Michael not only scored 32 points, but also threw a blanket over the high-scoring Isiah Thomas. But then Detroit rode Thomas' 33-point spree against Michael, who was weakened by the flu, to a win in game two. Thomas, though, wasn't interested in getting into a personal shoot-out against Michael. "If it's Isiah Thomas against Michael Jordan, I'm going to lose that battle every time."

It seemed as though the Pistons, who had built a substantial lead, were poised to put their game in gear and roll over the Bulls, but Michael threw a wrench into those plans by leading a furious rally that left the teams tied at 97 with only nine seconds left in the game. It was Michael time; time for Air Jordan to soar.

Michael took the inbounds pass and drove right against Dennis Rodman, a member of the NBA's All Defensive team. The move knocked Rodman off balance, and Michael went up for a short jump shot at the last second, though he had to twist his body while in the air to avoid Thomas, who had slid over to double-team him. But achieving the spectacular had become common-place for Michael the Magnificent, who flicked his wrist and watched the ball bank off the boards and into the basket with the winning points (his 45th and 46th points).

But it was the last win of the season for the outclassed Bulls. Detroit's ability to constantly harass and double-team Michael with fresh players from their deep bench finally took its toll. The Pistons were able to keep turning it on while the undermanned Bulls were just running down.

Although the Bulls had lost the series, 4–2, Michael's season had ended not in defeat, but in majesty. He had strapped an obviously inferior team to his back and through sheer will, enormous talent, and the most continuous display of clutch shooting in play-off history had taken it to within one step of the NBA championship series.

And Michael's awesome accomplishments certainly were recognized by the players around the league, who crowned his season by selecting him as the *Sporting News* Player of the Year for the second year in a row. And if basketball is ever played on other planets, he'll probably be named the Player of the Galaxy. As Lakers coach Pat Riley said, "If there was ever a person who walked out of an alien spaceship, it's Michael Jordan. He's the most outstanding player in professional basketball."

MICHAEL
JORDAN

(Chicago Bulls)

(Bill Smith, Chicago Bulls)

Top: Michael Jordan with Olympic gold and the victory net around his neck.

Bottom: Above the crowd.

Above: Michael driving to the basket.

Left: Michael closes in on Magic.

He really can fly!

Larry Bird is caught flat-footed
as Michael goes to the hoop.

MAGIC
JOHNSON

Top: Magic making a move on Larry Bird in NCAA finals.

Bottom: Magic gives Butch Lee a court-side bear hug after sixth game win over Sixers in 1980 championship series.

Top: Magic is airborne against Robert Reid.

Bottom: Magic drives to the hoop against Dale Ellis of the Super Sonics in 1987 playoff game.

(UPI/Bettman Newsphotos)

(UPI/Bettman Newsphotos)

Top: Greg Kite and Larry Bird try to cage Magic in 1987
finals . . .

Bottom: but Magic drove away with the MVP trophy and
the Jeep.

MAGIC JOHNSON

1

A Superstar is Coming

Earvin "Magic" Johnson was born August 14, 1959, in Lansing, Michigan. He was the second-oldest of eight children in a family of four boys (older brother Larry, and Quincey and Mike) and four girls (Pearl, Kim, Evelyn, and Evon).

With eight children to raise, the Johnson parents—Earvin, Sr., and Christine—had to work very hard to provide a good home. A large family like the Johnsons' required a lot of money just to feed and clothe. So Earvin, Sr., worked two and sometimes three jobs to give his family what they needed. Christine was also putting in a lot of overtime right in the house. And as soon as the youngest children were able to get along, Christine took a job in the Lansing school system.

When there are so many children in a family and the parents are working so hard, none of the children gets a lot of individual attention. But if the children have good parents, they learn at an early age how to take care of themselves and how to pitch in and help out. The older children were taught to help out with the younger children, and even the smallest ones learned to do simple chores at an early age. Children who grow up like this tend to grow up a little faster, accept responsibility a little sooner, and learn to take care of themselves while caring for others.

The Johnson children were lucky to have good and loving parents who created a close-knit, caring family. Little Earvin appreciated how hard his parents worked to provide a good home for the children, and he told his mother, "One day I'm going to make it, and I'll take care of you."

Despite the lack of minute-to-minute attention, the children were treated as individuals. As his mom points out, "One thing Earvin was taught was to be himself." And when the children demonstrated an ability at something, they were encouraged to pursue their talent. When young Earvin displayed an early attraction to music, his parents made sure that he had a small portable radio that he could carry around with him.

Earvin's early family life is probably responsible for providing him with the philosophy that underlies his approach to basketball: individual creativity at the service of the team, and doing whatever it takes to give the team the chance to win. And when Earvin grew up he still appreciated what a loving family means to an individual. "Kids should be close to their families because the family is always behind you."

Earvin displayed a fine singing voice at an early age, and his mother encouraged him to use it, thinking that he might have a career as a singer. But Earvin soon made it obvious that basketball would become the focal point of his life.

Both of Earvin's parents had been basketball players when they were growing up. Christine had played high-school ball back home in North Carolina, and Earvin, Sr., had played in his hometown of Brookhaven, Mississippi. When he had the time, Earvin, Sr., enjoyed watching the NBA Game of the Week on Sundays. And when the children joined him, he would use his basketball background to explain the fine points of the game. "When I started playing organized ball and the coach asked if anyone knew what a pick-and-roll is or how to run a three-man weave, I'd shoot right up," recalls Earvin.

By the time Larry was in fifth grade and Earvin was in fourth grade, they were getting up early on Sunday mornings to go one-on-one against each other in the nearby Main Street Elementary school playground. Earvin said that it was in those games that he first learned to dribble, because his older brother would press him all over the court. While they were playing, the brothers would often fantasize that they were basketball stars. Larry would pretend to be Walt Frazier, the slick-passing, sharp-shooting, ball-hawking guard who played for the New York Knicks. Earvin would pretend to be Wilt Chamberlain, the towering center of the Los Angeles Lakers.

Earvin loved playing basketball so much that when it snowed he would shovel the court so that he could practice. If no one else was available, he would practice by himself. It was in the playground that he met a boy named Jay Vincent, another youngster who shared Earvin's love for basketball. The two boys soon became best friends, never guessing how their paths would cross later on in their lives. When he could, Earvin played at the local Boys club, which was indoors and didn't need shoveling. When he was home, he would roll up socks and shoot them at imaginary baskets.

Earvin practiced because he loved to play and because it took a lot of talent to survive on the basketball courts in Lansing. There were always a lot more players than courts available, so if you didn't win, it was a long wait to get back on the court. That pressure to win caused most young players to neglect their outside shooting and concentrate instead on driving to the basket for easier-to-make layups. Driving to the basket in these early pickup games is how Earvin developed his "hoopsy doopsy" style.

By the time that Earvin was in fifth grade, he was almost six feet tall and was playing organized basketball. When he entered Dwight Rice Junior High School, he had reached six feet, and although he was very skinny, he played football as well as basketball.

While Earvin was at Dwight Rice he met Dr. Charles Tucker, a man who would play an influential role in his life. Dr. Tucker is a clinical psychologist and was a part-time instructor at Michigan State University as well as a psychological counselor for the Lansing school district. Dr. Tucker, who had played pro basketball for a year and a half, took an interest in Earvin, and Earvin was thrilled to actually know someone who had played pro ball.

When Earvin was still in the eighth grade, Dr. Tucker took him to a gym at Michigan State, where the college varsity played pickup games. "He'd get beat up by some of the MSU players," recalls Dr. Tucker, "but he finally learned to accept it as part of basketball. It is hard for young kids to learn that basketball is a contact sport and you have to get used to it."

In his first game at MSU, Earvin was befriended by Terry Furlow, who was the star of the Michigan State basketball team. Earvin looked up to Furlow, attracted as much by Terry's magnetic personality off the court as he was by his dynamic play on the court. Terry was fun and people liked to hang out with

45

him. And he took the eighth grader under his wing and referred to him as "my main man."

By the time Earvin was a ninth grader, he had grown to 6' 3" and his passing skills had already begun to attract notice. Earvin was expecting to go to Sexton High School, which was located about half a mile from his house on Middle Street, near the Oldsmobile factory where his father held a job. The neighborhood and the school were predominantly black. But the Lansing school board redistricted the city to bring about desegregation, and Earvin discovered that he would be attending Everett High School, which was about a mile and a half from his home and whose student body was mostly white.

Earvin wasn't very happy. "I was upset. I wanted to go to Sexton. I went to every Sexton game. I was a Sexton man, and then they came up with this busing thing." But George Fox, who was the basketball coach at Everett High, was delighted at the prospect of being able to coach a lot of talented black basketball players, especially Earvin. "He had a lot of talent even in junior high school. He wasn't a great outside shooter, but he had a great flair for the game. He wasn't a dominating player. He didn't like to go inside that much. He wasn't particularly fast, but he was quick. He had great anticipation and timing. He could jump, land and readjust with the best of them."

But it wasn't until that summer, right before Earvin would begin attending Everett, that Fox knew he was getting someone really special. Coach Fox watched Earvin play in the school yard and the Boys Club that summer and saw his abilities grow dramatically. "He really started to show us some things, and we started to get high on him. We knew we had a superstar coming."

46

2

The Biggest Dream

But Earvin made Coach Fox suck in his breath on the first day of
classes, when he found out that Earvin had gone out for football.
The coach didn't exhale until two days later, when Earvin
handed in his uniform. "I was very pleased," remembers Fox.
"He wasn't physically strong enough to play football."

Earvin didn't easily adjust to his new surroundings. It couldn't
have been easy to suddenly be attending a mostly white school
where previously he had attended almost all-black schools in an
almost all-black neighborhood. And a lot of teenagers just find
that time of life difficult. It can seem that your parents, especially, and the adult world in general, just don't understand. And it's
confusing having to answer to people when you think you're
pretty grown up and already know what's best for you. And
Earvin complicated matters by not applying himself to his
schoolwork. Coach Fox recalls that period, "I don't think Earvin
was as pleasant a person when I met him as he was after he
blossomed into a more mature individual. He was a little moody
and sulky and would become despondent over little things."

Earvin began to relax a bit when basketball practice began and
he met a teammate, Reggie Chastine. Reggie, who was a year
ahead of Earvin, played a style of ball similar to Earvin's. He
liked quarterbacking the team and hitting the open man. But
unlike Earvin, Reggie was only 5' 6 ", and he was loose and made
friends easily. Reggie's attitude helped Earvin to ease up.

Earvin couldn't wait to play his first high-school game; he
knew that once the season began, he would be in his element. But
when Earvin took the floor for his first game, he moved like a fish
out of water. "I choked. I didn't want to shoot. I didn't want to
dribble. I just wanted to pass the ball off to somebody else as
soon as I could. I think I fouled out in the third quarter. My
stomach was so tight."

But Magic settled down after that first game, and Everett jumped off to an 11–1 start, including a 71–47 shellacking of Sexton. Earvin was the team leader in scoring, rebounds, and assists. He brought the ball up and then played center. He was generating a lot of excitement in Lansing and drawing a lot of attention from the local press. After a particularly spectacular game against a tough Jackson High team in which Earvin recorded a triple double (36 points, 18 rebounds, and 14 assists) and stole the ball five times, one sportswriter, Fred Stabley, decided that Earvin needed a nickname that would describe his astonishing ability. "How do you like the name Magic?" Earvin smiled the super-bright sunshine smile that has become his trademark and said, "It's fine."

The Everett Vikings ended the season with a 20–1 overall record, going 12–0 in their league. They went on to take the district championship and the regional championship, but lost 58–55 in the quarterfinals of the state tournament after blowing a 13-point lead in the last quarter.

Magic wound up leading his team in points (22.3 per-game average), rebounding (16.9), assists, (138) blocked shots and steals. And Coach Fox pointed out something that isn't found in box scores but is just as important: "The best thing about him is his attitude. There's nothing he wouldn't do for the good of the team." When he was named to the All-State team, the first time that a sophomore had earned that distinction in the state of Michigan, Magic was thrilled. But he didn't let it go to his head. "I like the publicity, but it's not lasting unless you continue to live up to it. The only way to do that is to practice."

Magic earned money and got ready for the upcoming season by working at a basketball camp operated by Dr. Tucker. Whenever he wasn't teaching the younger boys, he was going one-on-one against Terry Furlow, who had been the top scorer in the Big Ten conference that past season.

By the time school started, Magic was 6'7". More importantly, he was comfortable with the other students, the faculty, and himself. He had a best friend in Reggie Chastine, and he loved playing basketball. Magic had improved his attitude toward his schoolwork because he knew he wouldn't be eligible to play basketball otherwise and because his parents insisted on passing grades. His mother was especially vigilant. "She didn't let him get away with *anything,*" Dr. Tucker remembers. His folks wanted him to go to college. With money being short and Magic big on basketball talent, they knew that a scholarship was in reach and invaluable. Magic also decided that college should be a part of his future. It would be a way for him to continue playing basketball, and he had become interested in pursuing a career in television journalism since becoming a reporter for the school newspaper.

The Everett Vikings dominated most of their opponents in the 1975–76 season, finishing with a 21–1 record, again going 12–0 in league play. During the season Magic set a single-game city scoring record when he pumped in 54 points against Sexton. In his very next game Magic realized that his shooting touch had deserted him, so he concentrated on his passing instead and chalked up 16 assists. After the game, he was asked which he liked more, scoring or playmaking. "The assists. I like to pass, hit the open man. I like to see somebody else enjoying it. They feel more like playing. Everybody likes getting his name in the paper."

The Vikings breezed through their first two games in the state tournament, but in the quarterfinals, playing in the same gym where they had squandered a 13-point lead the year before, they lost all but three points of a 15-point lead. With less than a minute to go, though, Magic whipped a full-court pass to a teammate who put in an easy layup to clinch the game. But the Vikings, who were the number-one-ranked team in the state, went no further. They were knocked out in the semifinals, 68–60, by an unranked team.

Magic had produced another banner year, leading the Vikings —by very wide margins—in points (25.8 per game), rebounds (170), assists (141), and steals (75). He averaged 33 points a game during the state tournament and was again named All-State, in addition to being chosen as All-Conference Most Valuable Player and UPI's Prep Player of the Year in Michigan.

With all of his individual awards, Magic was still disappointed that the Vikings hadn't captured the state title. He felt especially bad for Reggie Chastine, who wasn't going on to college and had lost his last chance for a championship. During that summer, though, Magic learned what real tragedy was when Reggie's young life was snuffed out in an automobile accident.

Before Magic began his senior year at Everett, hundreds of college coaches across the country had him in the number-one position on their wish list. One scouting service that a lot of teams subscribed to said: "This is the man! He's a 6'7", who plays like a 6'3", guard. Downtown shooting range, so effortless. Can pick a shot out of the air, then take it the length of the floor and score." The scouts also loved his aptitude for the game and the fact that he was a team player without an ego problem.

When the colleges actively began recruiting Magic, life in the Johnson home got very hectic, and the lives of Magic and his family became disrupted. His parents decided that the recruiters were intruding too much and that their son was too young to be under such a bright spotlight. So with Dr. Tucker's help, Magic and his family narrowed the choice to seven or eight schools, and the rest were sent polite rejection notices.

Magic really enjoyed his senior year. He had worked his way up to managing editor of the school newspaper and liked writing stories as well as selling advertising space to the local shopkeepers in Lansing. Magic was an active member of Lansing's Junior National Association for the Advancement of Colored People and a volunteer at a local Boys Club. In fact, Ron Dumke, the head of the Boys Club, thought so much of Magic's work that he nominated him for Boy of the Year. "I've never seen such openness, friendliness, and spirit of understanding. It's just unusual to find a young man who is having so much success, so willing to give his time to others. He's a super kid who is one fine human being."

Right before the basketball season began, Magic heard news that sent him racing through the corridors—the dunk shot, which had been outlawed for many years, was once again legal. Being allowed to stuff the ball would make playing the game more fun than ever. But as the team assembled for their first practice, Magic had something serious on his mind—Reggie Chastine. He and the team decided to dedicate themselves and their season to Reggie.

When the season started, Magic uncharacteristically was monopolizing the scoring. He was averaging 40 points a game, and while the Vikings were winning, Coach Fox was concerned that they couldn't win the state title as a one-man team. "I called him in and said, 'If we're going to win the state, you can't continue to play the way you're playing. You've got the entire crowd and all our opponents watching you, and that's fine. But you've also got four teammates watching you. You're going to start letting your teammates get involved.' Earvin just said, 'I got you, Coach,' and the next game he scored twelve points and had eighteen assists. That's the kind of kid he is."

For the third consecutive year the Vikings sailed through their season with only one loss. Then they romped through their first two games in the state tourney before earning a close victory in the semifinals. They had come close in each of the preceding two seasons but had come up a little short. This was Magic's last chance to take the title that he had dedicated himself to winning. The game played in Crisler Arena in Ann Arbor in front of a wildly cheering crowd of 13,609 was a tense, overtime struggle that the Vikings finally pulled out, 62–56, led by Magic's inspirational play and his 34 points, 14 rebounds, and four assists. The Vikings had finally taken the last step and captured the state title. Magic, who was named the tourney's MVP, was ecstatic. "This was my biggest dream. We've put three years of hard work into this and it means a lot," said Magic as his face broke into his sunshine smile. The Vikings' fans poured out of the stands and danced around the court with the players, yelling, "We're number one, we're number one!"

In the midst of the celebration, Magic remembered his friend Reggie Chastine and became quiet. "Reggie played a big part in my life, and that's why the team and I dedicated this state championship to him. Before each game this season we had one or two minutes of silence as a memorial to Reggie. I definitely feel he was a part of us winning the state title."

Magic finished his senior year with a 28.7 scoring average, 16.7 rebounds per game, 208 assists, and 99 steals, all team highs. His career total in points, 2,012 (good for a 26.0 average), and rebounds, 1,317 (good for a 17.0 average), established new city records in Lansing. He made the All-State team again, becoming the first player in Michigan ever to be chosen All-State three times. United Press International added to Magic's long list of awards by naming him the national Prep Player of the Year.

Now that his senior season was history, it was time for Magic to decide which college he wanted to attend. He paid a visit to four campuses and then, deciding it wasn't worth the hassle, cancelled an all-expenses-paid trip to Southern California to visit the UCLA campus. He was tired of all the attention and pressure, tired even of the limos and fancy restaurants. "At first you like it. You love it. It's a dream to be recruited. But after it gets going, it gets bad. There are constant telephone calls, and it gets to be a hassle."

Magic finally decided that he didn't want to go to a school that was too far from home, so he narrowed his choices to the University of Michigan, which is located about 60 miles from Lansing, in Ann Arbor, where the Vikings had won the state championship; and Michigan State, which is located in East Lansing, about three miles from the Johnson home. But the pressure on Magic remained intense. The people from Ann Arbor kept in constant contact with the Johnson household, and the people in Lansing let Magic know just how much they wanted him to stay home and play for Michigan State. People constantly stopped him in the street to offer their opinion, and more than 5,000 junior-high and high-school students signed a petition asking him to enroll at State.

Magic was able to escape the pressure in early spring when he went to Europe as part of a high-school all-star team to participate in the Albert Schweitzer Games. The games honor a very great man who dedicated his life to helping the poor and working for world peace. Magic enjoyed meeting people from other countries and cultures as well as getting to know his teammates from around the United States.

Magic expected that his family and, perhaps, a few reporters would meet him at the airport in Lansing when he returned. But when he stepped off the plane, he was overwhelmed to see about 400 people, including his high-school teammates and coach, the mayor of Lansing, and a couple of TV cameramen to record the whole scene. "I never expected anything like this," Magic told the crowd, many of whom were holding either Michigan or Michigan State signs. "It's super. It was a long trip and I'm glad to be home."

It was good to be home, but now Magic had to decide finally on a college. The University of Michigan was appealing because it was the defending Big Ten Conference champion and had a long tradition of success. Michigan State was appealing because Magic could play in front of his family and home town fans. His father really wanted him to go there; Magic might get more immediate playing time because the basketball program was weaker, and he would be reunited with his old playground buddy, Jay Vincent, who had already decided to attend MSU. At the end of April, Magic finally made his decision, and it made his dad, the basketball fans in Lansing, and Jeff Heathcote, the MSU coach, very happy. Magic was staying home.

Magic liked the idea of going to a school where he could help create a winning tradition. "I want to be there to help turn things around. We're going to go after a Big Ten championship next season." The fans wanted to be there too. The day after he declared his intent, long lines were formed at the ticket booths by people who wanted to be sure that they got tickets for the next season's games which was still five months away.

Magic had created a lot of pressure for himself by choosing to play in front of his home town fans and by promising to turn around the basketball program at lowly MSU. Magic, though, wasn't concerned. "I like pressure because I feel I can deal with it a lot better than most people. If you just play along with it and don't let it get to your head, don't let it affect your basketball game, then everything will be all right."

3

The Era of Earvin

Before Magic even put on a Spartan uniform, people were already proclaiming that he would create "The Era of Earvin" at MSU.

But before Magic began bouncing the ball, he settled in as a student. Although the Johnson home was very near the campus, Magic decided to live in a dormitory so that he could enjoy the full flavor of college life. When he registered for classes and saw how much he was going to have to read, he decided to sign up for a speed-reading course that the college offered. In discussing his reading ability at that time, Magic noted, "I think that was partly my fault and partly my high school's. I wasn't really reading back then. When I got in this class I had a very helpful teacher. She really mapped out some things that were helpful to me." And Magic, wanting to get off to a good start, followed the map well enough to compile a 3.4 grade-point average, which equals a B+, in his first semester.

Magic was really turned on to campus life. He liked meeting a lot of new people, and he enjoyed being a celebrity on campus, hearing people whisper, "Hey, that's Magic." He took a turn being a disc jockey at a local club and billed himself as "E.J. the DeeJay." And he really enjoyed spending Saturdays at the football stadium. "I love it," he beamed. "The students are so crazy and wonderful the way they have fun. College life is great."

Coach Heathcote wasn't predicting a Big Ten championship for the 1976–77 season, something that the Spartans hadn't managed since 1959, but he was optimistic about improving on the 10–17 record and sixth-place finish recorded a year earlier. In addition to Magic and Jay Vincent, Coach Heathcote was looking to Greg Kelser, a star forward, and senior guard Robert Chapman.

The starting five gave Coach Heathcote good reason to feel

positive about the upcoming season, but he was worried that the other players, especially Kelser, who had been a star himself since high school, might resent all the publicity being showered on the newcomer. But Kelser wasn't just an excellent basketball player; he was also a mature young man who put the team in front of his own ego. He had met Magic at a party a few years earlier and liked what he had seen. "I was impressed right away because he was getting all kinds of press when he was fifteen and it didn't swell his head. He was very mature for his age. I realized Earvin was a super player when he came, and I figured if we started to win, everything would work out."

The expectations on campus were so high that the Spartans' practices were drawing more fans than had come to see actual games the preceding year. Everyone was really excited about the opening game. Jenison Field House, the Spartans' home arena, was sold out. The newspapers had Magic's name in headlines and his picture on the front page. It was showtime. It was time for the Magic Man to perform.

But when the game began, the star developed stage fright. He turned the ball over seven times in the first half. While he settled down later on and produced decent stats—seven points, nine rebounds, eight assists—the opening-night performance failed to live up to its promise. Magic didn't dodge or alibi; he just told it straight. "I was scared. Early in the game when I went up to shoot, I didn't want to shoot. I had cramps in my stomach. But when we needed a pass for a basket, I thought I played well under the pressure. I'll get better. I feel bad because of the way I played, but I feel good because we won."

Magic got better very quickly, and he felt good most of the time because the Spartans won most of the time. They traveled to Syracuse for four days to play in the Carrier Classic tournament. The Spartans won the first game, then dropped a close one to Syracuse in the finals, but Magic went home with the tourney's MVP trophy. The Spartans came home for their fourth game, against Wichita State, and Magic put on a show as he hit for 19 points, nine assists, and a whopping 20 rebounds, missing a triple double by one assist. Magic was pumped up. "There's absolutely no feeling in the world like coming out at the start of a game. You can smell the popcorn, see the fans, and when that band strikes up the fight song, you just want to jump up and touch the ceiling. I get so fired up before each game. Wow, what an experience!"

Watching Magic perform his mastery on a basketball court was also a "wow" experience. Coach Heathcote, who enjoyed a front-court seat, could fully appreciate the show. "His tremendous court sense allows him to pass to the open man at the right time, and that's an art. In Earvin's case you don't just talk about the points he scores, but the points he produces. Not just the buckets and assists, but the first pass that makes the second pass possible. He's the best player on the open court today." And he was only a freshman!

When a reporter again asked Kelser if he resented all the attention that was being lavished on Magic, Greg replied, "All I know is that we were one and four at this time last year without Earvin, and we're four and one this season with him. But I really have to keep my eye on Earvin, because some of his great passes make me look silly when I'm not expecting them." Greg and Magic went on to become extremely close friends, as did their dads. So close, in fact, that Magic said, "Greg is like a brother to me."

The Spartans got on a roll and won 13 straight, a school record, and were ranked among the top ten college teams in the country. After Magic led MSU past Michigan for the first time since 1973, the Wolverine coach tipped his hat. "Johnson plays forward, guard, center, and coaches a little. And he doesn't do a bad job. The Pistons would be smart to draft him. He'd fill that Silverdome in Pontiac. They're throwing all that money around to people who can't play. They might as well give it to a player. He's a great player. I'd like to see him turn pro."

The Wolverine coach may have been wishing that Magic would turn pro just so he wouldn't have to try to defense him for three more years. But rumors *were* circulating that Detroit was interested in drafting Magic. With his great talent and fan appeal, especially in Michigan, it would be a natural. Magic was thinking about it too, but he told reporters he wouldn't talk about it until after the Spartans had finished their season. He didn't want anything to upset the team's concentration.

The team kept concentrating and kept winning, finishing the regular season at 25–5, the first time in its 79-year history that a Spartan team had won as many as 20 games. Magic's skills had led the way, and his enthusiasm had set the tone that made it all possible. "We entered every game, home and away, with the idea that we were going to win. When you feel that way and play hard, it's tough to lose."

Magic had promised that the Spartans would go after the Big Ten title, and they not only went after it, they grabbed it! The first-place finish provided the Spartans with automatic entry into the NCAA tournament, the dream of every college team. The Spartans kept the dream alive until they were knocked off by the number-one-ranked Kentucky Wildcats in the regional finals. Magic, who had led the Big Ten in assists and had tied for third in scoring and sixth in rebounding, did not shine like a star in the tournament, and he blamed himself for the loss. "My whole tournament was bad. I don't know any reason for it. I just tried to do other things when my shots wouldn't fall."

Magic may have had played poorly in postseason play, but that didn't cool the interest of the Detroit Pistons. So it was decision time again. Turn pro or stay in school. Everyone seemed to have an opinion and offer advice. It was a lot for an eighteen-year-old to deal with.

Magic's parents wanted him to remain in school. His mom wanted him to stay and continue working toward a degree. His dad, with Dr. Tucker's help, checked out the amount of money that would be offered and decided it wasn't enough to cause his son to leave college. He also thought that Magic would benefit from playing another year of college ball.

After all the advice was in, though, it was still Magic's decision to make, and after twisting and turning about it, he decided that he would stay in school. "It was the hardest decision I ever had to make. Choosing a college was small stuff compared to what I've been going through the last couple of weeks. I really wanted to enter the draft. It wasn't so much the fact of all that money as it was finally being able to realize the dream of being a professional that I've had so long."

Magic had postponed his dream of playing professional basketball, but he did get to spend his summer traveling through Europe with a college all-star team. He enjoyed the games and the new people that he met. One of his teammates, a tall, blond forward, was someone whose path he would continue to criss-cross as though they were linked by some invisible thread. The teammate's name was Larry Bird.

When Magic returned to campus as a sophomore, he concentrated on his schoolwork even though he knew he might turn pro at the end of the school year. He had greatly improved his reading speed and ability through the special class he had begun as a freshman, and he signed up for it again. He took a full credit load, studied three to four hours a day, and kept his mind strictly on his life at MSU. "I can't be in there half stepping: halfway going pro and halfway in college. I'm all the way in college now, and I have to treat it like that."

Magic's sophomore season got off to a splashy start, as he was featured on the cover of *Sports Illustrated* magazine wearing a tuxedo. There were also photos inside the magazine showing Magic on a court taking shots while wearing the tux, a top hat, and black-leather shoes. The magazine's point was that college basketball was "classy."

And the Spartans were preseason picks to finish near the top of the class. They had five of their top six players returning from the past season and received valuable experience practicing against teams in Brazil. Coach Heathcote thought they were strong enough to reach the NCAA finals. "I told the players it will take five things for us to win. In order, they are: teamwork, the fast break, defense, field-goal-shooting accuracy, and offense. I let Earvin take care of the first two, and I handle the rest." To further demonstrate his faith in Magic's leadership qualities, Coach Heathcote named him a cocaptain, an unusual honor for an underclassman.

The Spartans started the season smartly but then went into a serious midseason slump. Coach Heathcote moved Magic from point guard to forward to bolster the team's rebounding and stop

58

the slide. But when Ohio State invaded Jenison Field House, the Spartans still trailed the Buckeyes by four games in the Big Ten Conference. It was a must game for MSU if they had any hope of repeating as Big Ten champions and insuring a berth for themselves in the upcoming NCAA tournament.

The Spartans played superbly in the first half behind Magic's manipulations and built up a solid nine-point lead. But right before the intermission, Magic went down, writhing in pain from an ankle sprain. Without Magic in the lineup, the Buckeyes bounced back in the second half. The Big Ten championship and the NCAA tournament bid were slipping through the Spartans' grasp as their injured star lay in the locker room. But then, with less than ten minutes left in the game, Magic hobbled out to the MSU bench. "I had great pain, but I knew I had to block it out and go back out there and play. The doctors and trainers had already made up their minds that I wasn't going to play, but I told them if we lost this game, there was no tomorrow."

As Magic limped over to the scorer's table, the MSU fans let loose a thunderous ovation. "It made me want to cry." But after Magic led the Spartans to an 84–79 victory, it was the Buckeyes who were shedding the tears. "Earvin showed a lot of guts," noted Coach Heathcote. "But when it's winning time, it's playing time."

With Magic and Greg Kelser leading the way, the Spartans kept right on winning. Their favorite play was the alley-oop play, with Magic lobbing a pass to Greg right above the basket so that Greg could go up, grab the ball, and slam-dunk it all in one smooth motion. The play, which calls for perfect timing, fires up a team and excites the crowd. "A little eye contact is all we need," explained Kelser. "I know what he's looking for, and he knows what I'm looking for." What they were both looking for was the NCAA championship, and they took a big step in that direction by leading the Spartans to a 21–6 record and a share of the Big Ten title.

The Spartans roared through the early stages of the tournament like a high-speed express train. In the first round they beat Lamar, 95–64, behind Magic's ten assists and Greg's 31 points. Next they rode Magic's 24 points and 12 assists to a joyride over

LSU. And then they took the regional by beating top-seeded Notre Dame, as Greg scored 34 points and Magic dished out 13 assists.

The train kept going, right to the University of Utah Sports Center and the Final Four. The Final Four is a spectacular sports spectacle, mixing the best parts of Super Bowl Sunday and the Barnum & Bailey Circus. It's a beautiful riot of color and noise, of cheerleaders and marching bands and wildly cheering fans. And the air crackles with electricity as the Final Four teams go for the ultimate dream.

The Spartans raced by their semifinal opponent, the University of Pennsylvania, as if the Quakers were a whistlestop in the middle of nowhere. By halftime the Spartans led 50–17, and they kept the pedal to the floor and roared to an astonishing 101–34 victory, behind Magic's triple double (29 points, ten rebounds, and ten assists).

The Spartans were one stop away from the championship now. But standing in their path was Indiana State University, the top-ranked team in the country. The undefeated Sycamores were led by a big, blond All-American forward named Larry Bird.

It was a dream matchup featuring the two best players in college basketball. The media tried to create a rivalry between the two superstars, but they wouldn't cooperate. "I've been on the same floor with Bird. We threw each other some nice passes. We had some fun. He's a good guy, great," said Magic. And Larry returned the compliment. "Earvin Johnson is probably one of the best players I ever played with."

The two stars and the two teams had entirely different approaches to the big game. Magic, as usual, was having a great time. He was upbeat and extroverted, encouraging his teammates and providing good copy for the legion of reporters covering the game. Bird, who approached the game with a quiet intensity, was aware of the contrast between the two superstars. "To me, it's very serious. I can't be laughing like he does out there. I just hope when it's over, he ain't laughing at me."

The teams had to approach the game with different strategies as well. The Sycamores had to be concerned with two major

60

threats, Magic and Greg Kelser, but they couldn't overplay Magic too much or he would hit the open man for easy buckets. In preparing for Indiana State, essentially a one-man team, the idea was to cage Bird, harass him with multiple defenses, and deny him the ball as much as possible and double- and triple-team him as soon as he touched it. The idea behind the strategy was simple enough, but given the Sycamores' 32–0 record and Bird's 30-point scoring average, it was obvious that no team had been successful in getting the theory to work on the court.

But the inspired Spartans made it work. They bottled up the Sycamores' offense by clogging up the passing lanes and denying Bird the ball. "He was very frustrated," reported Jay Vincent. "He kept saying, 'Give me the ball, give me the ball,' but his teammates couldn't get it to him."

The Spartans opened the second half with three straight hoops to stretch their lead to 42–28, and the MSU fans began to chant, "We're number one, we're number one!" When the final whistle sounded, Magic and Greg Kelser stood under a basket and hugged each other as the MSU fans swarmed all over the court.

Magic was in basketball heaven. But as his eyes swept around the arena, he caught a glimpse of Larry Bird, crying into a towel, and for a moment he remembered how he had felt when Everett High had twice been eliminated from the state tournaments.

But Magic, who had scored a game-high 24 points, was quickly swept back up in the exhilaration of having achieved a cherished dream. And his sense of accomplishment was completed when it was announced that he had been named the tournament's MVP. When Magic was asked if he was surprised that the Spartans had toppled the Sycamores, he replied, "I always set my sights high. I don't aim to be second best in anything I do, and I really felt we could win the national championship one day."

Now that the season was over, it was decision time again for Magic. He would have to decide whether to remain in school or begin his pro career, and there were strong pulls in both directions. His mother let him know that she would prefer it if he would stay in school and get his degree. And Magic enjoyed campus life and the fun and excitement of college basketball. As Jay Vincent said to his old playground buddy, "What's better than that?" And if Magic kept his amateur status for another year, he would be eligible for the 1980 Olympics. The basketball fans in Lansing and throughout Michigan certainly made Magic's decision more difficult by showing how much they appreciated him. One man even went so far as to spend $1,200 to place an ad in *The Michigan State News* that urged Magic to stay by explaining the lifetime value of a college education.

But Magic had fulfilled his ambitions in the college game, and he wanted to test his talent in the NBA. He decided that if the price was right, he would turn pro. His big concern was making his mother comfortable with his decision, which he did by promising her that he would complete his college studies in the off-seasons.

The Los Angeles Lakers owned the rights to the number-one selection in the 1979 college draft, and they made no secret of the fact that Magic was the man they wanted. The Lakers made the price right—$600,000 over four years—and the deal was done.

The first thing that Magic wanted to do was rush out and buy a new house and special presents for his family. But his parents, who had worked so hard for so long, with help from Dr. Tucker and Magic's agent, Charles Andrews, explained to Magic the wisdom of investing his money wisely and letting it work for him so that he could have financial security for the rest of his life.

On draft day Magic sat in the Grand Ballroom of the elegant Plaza Hotel in New York City. He had come a long way in a short time. In just two years he had gone from leading his high-school team to a state title to leading his college team to the NCAA championship. He had traveled to foreign countries and grown tremendously as a person. And now the little boy who had shoveled snow to play at being Wilt Chamberlain was going to Los Angeles, where it never snows, to play on the same hardwood court that Wilt had dominated a generation earlier. As the Lakers announced his selection, Magic smiled his beautiful sunshine smile and thought, "Wow, I'm on the same team with Kareem."

4

Show Time

In the summer Magic flew out to Los Angeles and bought an apartment for himself. His mother was concerned that the wrong kind of people would try to get their claws into Magic, a young, wealthy man in a fast city, living alone for the first time. But Magic had too much sense and was too dedicated to basketball to waste his time or his body on partying into the early morning or messing with drugs. Magic immediately joined an NBA rookie league to stay in shape and begin adapting to the pro game.

Magic knew that there was a big difference between college ball and the NBA. The players are bigger and stronger and much more talented. And the longer schedule and the constant traveling becomes a grind and wears a body down. But he was looking forward to the challenge.

And the fans in Los Angeles were looking forward to watching him play. A big crowd came to watch his first game in the rookie league, and Magic gave the fans a show by pumping in 24 points and handing out nine assists.

When Magic showed up at the Lakers' training camp, he was a bit apprehensive. He had heard that some of the veteran players were cool and aloof, and he wondered how they would react to his emotional approach to the game. But he decided to just do his best, be himself, and see what happened.

Magic showed up at the first workout with a large tape player and some rock-and-roll tapes. "It weighs a lot," he acknowledged, "but I *have* to have it. It just relaxes you, gets you ready to play. You bounce around, get your feet tappin', and you're ready to go."

Magic was ready to go right away, but it took a while for him and his teammates to adjust to each other. In the beginning Magic would throw passes to where he thought players should be moving and then watch as the ball bounced into empty space. Or he would throw a no-look pass to an unsuspecting teammate and see it bounce off his body. "I hit a lot of people in the face, and I got a lot of turnovers, but I just worked on it until I got it right."

One of the ways that Magic worked on it was to spend time watching his teammates on the floor to learn their moves and habits. Gradually it began to come together as his teammates adapted and came to expect the unexpected. They found out that if they got a step on a defender, Magic would find a way to get them the ball from anywhere on the court. And knowing that they would get the ball if they were open made them work harder to get open and made the Lakers a more dangerous team. Veteran power forward Jim Chones explained that unique aspect of Magic's game. "He uses angles a lot of players don't see, and he gives you the ball in the rhythm of your move so you can go right up with it."

Magic had held back a bit in the beginning, controlling his flow of emotions on the court. But as he began to feel like a part of the team, his naturally buoyant personality bubbled up to the surface. He began to talk more, offer encouragement to his teammates, and run them down and slap them five whenever they made a sharp play.

Initially his teammates didn't know what to make of this cocky rookie with the rah-rah style and the beautiful smile. "At first we couldn't believe him," said Jamaal Wilkes, a graceful forward with a deadly shot. "He was *so* enthusiastic. We weren't sure it was genuine. But it was. That's him. That's Magic." And the irrepressible rookie had performed a trick equal to any magician's sleight of hand; he had brought the spirit of college basketball into the professional arena. In fact the Lakers began calling him Buck, a nickname that they felt captured the energy and enthusiasm that he brought to the game.

The Lakers still hadn't worked out all the kinks by the time of their season opener on October 12. They had six new players on the team and a rookie coach, Jack McKinney, trying to bring it all together. But the people in LA were excited about the opportunity to see their new star perform in his first pro game, and more than 17,000 fans filled the Forum.

Their expectations quickly turned to disappointment, though, and Magic's dream descended into nightmare. The Magic Man wasn't wowing anyone, and the only thing that disappeared was his game. "I was in another world," he acknowledged, after scoring a single point in seventeen minutes. "The coach took me out, and it was a good thing he did."

It was like his first game at Everett and MSU all over again. But this time when he went back in, he quickly got his act together and lit up the scoreboard for 26 points. Kareem Abdul-Jabbar gave the game a happy ending by sinking a last-second sky hook to give the Lakers a 103–102 victory over the Clippers.

Magic was so excited about winning his first game that he ran straight over to Kareem and startled him with a bear hug. "It's hard for me to keep my emotions inside," Magic explained. "I want to express them *now*. That's what a team is all about."

A month into the season Coach McKinney suffered a serious head injury when he fell off his bicycle and had to be replaced by his assistant, Paul Westhead. Magic and his teammates were upset by the accident, but they didn't miss a beat. The very next night they hosted the Denver Nuggets. The game went into overtime and Magic went into overdrive. He ripped the nets for eight straight buckets on his way to a 31-point, six-rebound, eight-assist performance that led the Lakers to a 126–122 victory.

Magic continued to weave his spell, and in one torrid stretch in the second month of the season he *averaged* triple-double numbers: 29.6 points, 11.6 rebounds, and 11.3 assists. That streak earned him his first NBA Player of the Week award. Dennis Johnson, who was a star guard for the Seattle Supersonics at the time, quickly became a believer. "What impresses me most is his intelligence. He recognizes situations on the court very well. For any young player to come into this league and understand what's going on as well as he does is amazing."

Word spread quickly about the stylish way that Magic ran the Lakers, dribbling the ball as if it were on a string and throwing no-look passes through traffic for easy baskets. Attendance picked up dramatically, and Hollywood actors and actresses and sports personalities began paying regular visits to the Forum. Magic was delighted to meet the famous people and was always surprised to discover that they were excited about meeting him. One night O.J. Simpson walked into the locker room, and Magic said, "Hi, what's happening?" O.J. pointed at the smiling young man and said, "*You're* what's happening."

Magic had the Lakers running and winning. They had developed an exciting style and a new attitude. It became known as Show Time. "When we're rolling and the break is going, I guess it looks like I am performing magic out there. There are some nights I think I can do anything. You really have to love the game to play that way, though. You can't be afraid to let your emotions out in front of thirteen thousand people."

Even the great Kareem, a seasoned veteran at 31, had been revitalized. "Magic does so many unbelievable things on the court that you work harder to make his plays pay off. It's great to play with him."

And Kareem, whom Magic calls "Big Fella," was like a big brother to the rookie. He helped him adjust to life in the NBA and was always there to provide Magic with off-the-court advice as well.

By midseason the Lakers were only one game out of first place in the Pacific Division, and they had the fourth-best record in the NBA. But then Magic began to take too much on himself and got away from working within the team concept. Pat Riley, who was then the assistant coach, took Magic aside and talked to him in much the same way that George Fox had done when Magic began his senior year at Everett by averaging 40 points per game. Riley reminded Magic that if he didn't use his teammates, he would lose them. They would stop working, start standing around, and become spectators at the Magic Show. They would also resent the rookie's showing a lack of confidence in their ability to perform and acting as if his skills were vastly superior to their own.

At first Magic reacted negatively to Riley's words. But then the message quickly sunk in. Magic realized that his role wasn't to perform as a solo act but to give the team direction and to control the flow of the game. "My whole game is court sense, being smart, taking charge, setting up a play, or, if I have to, scoring."

Magic snapped out of his funk, turned up the meter on his enthusiasm, and got the Lakers' motor humming. He still made mistakes occasionally, and sometimes his passes were too creative for his teammates to handle, but his ability and his upbeat attitude kept the Lakers rolling. "Magic has such an infectious, happy attitude that he's imparted it to the other players," noted Laker owner Jerry Buss. "They're happy while they're playing, and they're very intent on winning."

Magic's high-voltage performance turned on the entire league, and when the ballots were counted, they showed that he was the first rookie in eleven years to be named a starter in an NBA All-Star game.

Magic led the Lakers on a late-season surge that allowed them to leapfrog over the Seattle Supersonics, the defending NBA champs, and take first place in the Pacific Division. Their 60–22 record was the second best in the entire league, and the first-place finish was especially sweet for the Laker veterans who had been knocked out of the playoffs by the Sonics the preceding two seasons.

Magic's season-ending statistics and the Lakers' first-place finish offered a vivid picture of his unique talents and ability to provide leadership. He averaged 18.0 points a game with a fine .530 field-goal percentage, the best ever for a Laker rookie. He handed out 563 assists, another Laker rookie record, and he pulled down 7.7 rebounds per game, the second-highest number ever recorded in the NBA by a guard. He was a unanimous choice for the All-Rookie team, and finished second to Larry Bird in the voting for Rookie of the Year. More than one NBA observer thought that it would have been appropriate if they had shared the award.

The Lakers made short work of their opening-round opponents in the 1980 playoffs, disposing of the Phoenix Suns four games to one. And they doused Seattle's dream of repeating as league champions by eliminating the Sonics by the same four-to-one margin. Those triumphs earned Los Angeles a trip to the

NBA finals for the first time since 1973. Their opponents were the high-flying Philadelphia 76ers, who had advanced to the finals by beating Boston. The 76ers were led by Julius Erving, the incomparable Dr. J.

The teams split the first two games at the Forum. The Lakers took the first one, 109–102, behind Kareem, who scored a game-high 33 points and hauled down 14 rebounds, and Magic, who just missed a triple double with 16 points, ten assists, and nine rebounds. After the Sixers took the second game, 107–104, the series moved to the Spectrum in Philadelphia, where the Lakers hadn't won since 1975. And their task was made that much more difficult when Coach Westhead suspended strong forward Spencer Haywood for disciplinary reasons. But the Lakers surprised the Sixers in the third game, 111–101, before dropping the fourth, 105–102, despite a 28-point performance from Magic.

The teams flew back to Los Angeles for game five, and they made it a memorable one. With the Lakers leading by two points in the third quarter, Kareem went up for a rebound, and as he came down, he became tangled in a crowd of players and fell to the floor. Kareem was immediately taken out of the game, his left ankle severely sprained. Even though Magic was a rookie and only 20 years old, he decided to take charge. "I wanted the ball. I wanted to take over. We knew we couldn't get our heads down with Kareem injured. The team had to keep playing basketball and get more intense."

With Magic controlling the flow and creating opportunities, the Lakers pushed their lead up to eight points at the end of the third quarter. In the fourth quarter Kareem made a dramatic return. Playing despite great pain, he poured in 14 of his game-high 40 points, including a three-point play that snapped a 103–103 tie with 33 seconds left in the game as the Lakers prevailed, 108–103.

Kareem had provided the points and the inspiration for victory in game five, but the injury was so severe that he couldn't accompany the Lakers back to Philadelphia for game six.

Magic decided to wear Kareem's number 33 on his jersey instead of his own 32 and to dedicate the game to the Big Fella.

The injury to his friend had taken the smile from Magic's face. There was no smile, but there was no surrender either. In order to bolster the front court, which was depleted by the absence of Kareem and Haywood, Coach Westhead made an inspired move—he decided to start Magic in Kareem's spot at center. In the locker room he told the players, "Everybody expects us to be courageous tonight. We're not here to be courageous; we're here to win."

The Sixers were surprised when Magic went out to take the center jump at the start of the game. They were surprised, and he was confused. "I didn't know whether to stand with my right foot forward or my left. I didn't know when I should jump or where I should tap it if I got it. I looked at Caldwell Jones, the Seventy-sixers' center, and realized he's seven-one and he's got arms that make him around nine-five. So I just decided to jump up and down quick, then work on the rest of my game."

Magic went to work and created a masterpiece, producing one of the most remarkable performances in playoff history. He was all over the floor, pumping in points, sweeping the boards, hitting the open man, and harassing the 76er offense. When the final whistle blew, the Lakers had the game, 123–107, and the NBA championship. And Magic had made it all possible by putting together an astonishing line: 42 points on 14 of 23 shots from the floor and a perfect 14 for 14 from the free-throw line; 15 rebounds; seven assists; three steals; and one blocked shot. (Some people claim to have seen him selling popcorn during timeouts.)

When the television crew came onto the floor to interview him after the game, Magic smiled his best sunshine smile and sent a message to an injured friend. "Big Fella, I did it for you. I know your ankle hurts, but I want you to get up and dance." And three thousand miles away, Kareem sat in front of his television and laughed.

Magic had come up bigger than anyone could have guessed or expected. He had played every position on the court full out for 47 minutes while pushing his talents and his stamina to their limits. Magic's masterly performance earned him the Most Valuable Player award for the championship series.

In the space of four seasons, from high school to the NBA,

Magic had led three teams to championships and won three MVP awards doing it. It seemed that every time the merry-go-round went around, Magic grabbed a brass ring.

The team flew back to Los Angeles for a victory celebration, and then Magic was on his way to New York to pick up his MVP prize. He slowed down long enough to agree to endorse Converse and Spalding products and do some modeling. Then it was back home to Lansing, to being one of the guys and playing softball, which Magic loves to do, and back to MSU to take courses, as he had promised his mother he would do. And back to relax and recoup from his whirlwind season. It had been a season to remember and to savor. Or, as Magic put it, "This season—wow! —ninety-seven games. Exciting. Crazy. Fun. A lot of love for each other. A great experience. I learned a lot and—we're the world champs. Wow!"

There was one sad note, though. During the same week that Magic was winning the championship and the MVP award, Terry Furlow, the former MSU star who had befriended Magic when Magic was still in junior high, died when he crashed his car at 3 A.M. on a lonely Ohio road. Tests performed after the crash established that both Valium and cocaine were in Furlow's bloodstream at the time of the crash. Terry had not lived up to his, or anyone else's, expectations in the NBA. So this charismatic man, who had always been the best and most popular person, turned to drugs as a crutch to ease the pain. His pain stopped at 3 A.M. on a lonely, dark road.

5

Mixed Bag

Magic's second season got off to a sensational start. He was relaxed, secure in his role, and aware of his value to the Lakers. With Magic leading the way, LA quickly raced out to a 15–5 record. Magic was leading the league in steals and assists. He was the Lakers' leading scorer, with a 22.4 average (tenth best in the league), and their second-leading rebounder. And then it all came to a screeching halt—as Magic crumpled to the floor. The cartilage in his knee had been badly torn, and within a week he was in surgery.

The recovery period was slow, and the inactivity hung heavy on the 21-year-old. Initially the Lakers sputtered in his absence, losing five of their next nine games. But then they began to regroup as Magic began the difficult task of building back the strength in his knee. Six days a week he went to a room and lifted weights with the leg. Lying down on his back, he pumped the leg up and down as though he were riding a bicycle. It was difficult and monotonous work. "Now I know how a factory worker feels." As soon as he could, Magic took a seat on the team bench at the Forum and cheered the team on. But the injury and the idleness were getting Magic down.

The recovery, including time back in Lansing, where Dr. Tucker helped Magic build up his strength, took three and a half months. As soon as the Lakers announced the date of Magic's return, the game became a sellout, and fans began sporting buttons that read, "The Magic is back."

But Magic's knee wasn't thoroughly healed, and it wasn't easy for him or the team to try and get in sync with each other after such a long absence. They made it into the playoffs but were humbled by the Houston Rockets, two games to one. Magic was horrendous in the final game, sinking just two of 13 from the field; but with fifteen seconds left and the Rockets up by one point, he had an opportunity for redemption. Magic was supposed to get the ball in to Kareem for a sky hook, but he couldn't find a passing lane to the Big Fella this time. So he drove the lane himself, but just as he went up for the shot, Moses Malone jumped out at him and caused an air ball. End of game, end of season.

It had been a tough season for Magic to endure. The injury and the early elimination were painful. But what concerned Magic the most was the lack of chemistry on the team. "The trouble is, we became a team of individuals this season. We had some guys who became more interested in 'I' than 'we'"

During the off-season Jerry Buss, the Lakers' owner, surprised Magic and stunned the sports world. He signed his young star to a new contract that would pay Magic one million dollars a year for the next *25 years.* "The thought of not having Magic with the Lakers is unthinkable. He's a fantastic player and a great person. I want to keep him in Los Angeles forever. I expect another ten years in uniform; then he'll work for me. He could coach; he could run the team; he could even run the business."

Magic reported to training camp in good spirits, satisfied with his contract and determined to lead the Lakers back to the top. But Magic, and most of the other players, quickly became unhappy when Coach Westhead restructured the Lakers' offense. Westhead wanted to curtail the running game and have the team play a disciplined, half-court game instead. Magic tried to persuade Westhead that the Lakers needed to run and play more creatively. The Lakers' game had gone from Show Time to Slow Time, but the coach wouldn't budge. Magic became totally frustrated and told reporters that he couldn't play for Westhead. He wanted to be traded. "I can't play here anymore. I'm not happy now. I haven't been all season."

Buss had realized that the team was being pulled apart and that the situation was unworkable. He had decided on a solution before Magic's outburst, and the next day he put his plan into action. He announced that Westhead had been fired and replaced by assistant coach and former Laker player Pat Riley.

Magic and many of the other players were thrilled, because

they believed that the team would now be able to play up to its potential.

But a lot of basketball people in Los Angeles and around the country who weren't aware of the facts blamed Magic for Westhead's firing. The media was full of stories about Magic being an overpaid, spoiled brat who had thrown a temper tantrum. And the fans regularly rained down a shower of boos whenever Magic took the floor. They didn't know that Magic had tried to act in the best interests of the team. And most of them remained unforgiving, despite the fact that the Lakers went off on a 17–3 tear.

The situation had a big effect on Magic. "I couldn't even listen to the radio. But even tougher than all that was the booing. That just made me *play*. That made me have my best year. I figured, they're booing, so I just have to go to work now.

"I didn't regret what I did or said. It made me a better person, made me mature. It made me grow up. That's the main thing. Some good can come from something like that. I learned a lot from it, no question."

By the end of the season, though, Magic had transformed most of the boos into cheers with his dazzling all-around play. He led the league in steals (2.67 per game), was second in assists (9.5), and joined Hall of Famers Wilt Chamberlain and Oscar Robertson as the only players in the history of the NBA ever to register 700 or more points, rebounds, and assists in one season.

The Lakers steamed into the playoffs and swept the Suns and the San Antonio Spurs to advance easily to the championship round against the 76ers again. It was the first time that any NBA team had ever accomplished consecutive four-game sweeps.

The first two games were played at the Spectrum, and the teams split them. The Lakers won the opening game, becoming the first team ever to win nine consecutive playoff games. And the Sixers took the second game. It was the Lakers' first loss in nearly seven weeks!

Magic led the Lakers to two wins at the Forum, and the teams traveled back to the Spectrum with the Lakers hoping to close out the Series. The Sixers, though, wouldn't cooperate, as they trounced the Lakers by 33 points. But the Lakers snapped back behind Magic's steady all-around performance—13 points, 13 rebounds, and 13 assists—to take their second NBA championship in three seasons. After the game Pat Riley went over to Magic, hugged him, and said, "Thanks." Magic finished his emotionally charged season on a high note by capturing his second championship-series MVP award.

Before the 1982–83 season began, Magic had one major goal—to have the Lakers repeat as NBA champions, something that no team had been able to do since the Celtics had done it in 1969.

During the regular season Magic just missed repeating his triple in the "700 club" when he snared only 683 rebounds. Ironically, his 8.6 rebound average was the best figure for a guard that season. He led the league in assists, with a 10.5 average, and his total of 823 broke the Lakers' team record, which had been held by Jerry West, a Hall-of-Fame guard who is now the Lakers' general manager.

Magic continued to show his great versatility and dedication to the team by racking up the triple doubles (achieving double figures—ten or more—in the three categories of points, rebounds, and assists).

He clicked for 16 triple doubles in the 79 games he played and added 35 double doubles. He showed that he would work every facet of his game—dish out assists, bang the boards for rebounds, and score points when necessary—in the pursuit of Laker victories rather than selfishly inflate his own scoring average.

Kareem's scoring led the Lakers past Portland in the opening round of the 1983 playoffs, four games to one. Kareem stayed hot against San Antonio while Magic *averaged* triple-double figures —17.5 points, 10.5 rebounds, and 14 assists—and the Lakers knocked off the Spurs, four games to two.

The Lakers, though, went into the finals against the Sixers seriously undermanned. James Worthy suffered a season-ending injury a week before the playoffs began. They suffered additional injuries during the final round and faced an incredible performance by the ex-Rocket Moses Malone, and were swept 4–0.

Magic was disappointed that the Lakers hadn't repeated,

hadn't even challenged in the finals. It was time to head back to Lansing, to his mother's home cooking, the softball team, and summer school at MSU.

Magic also devoted a lot of time to charities, something he does on a regular basis. He has helped raise money to fight sickle-cell anemia, and for the Special Olympics, among others. And he began a program in Lansing called Action Reading, which aids local students with reading problems.

6

Big Times in Beantown

Magic and the rest of the team began the season with one goal: to make up for the embarrassment of being swept by the Sixers. They took their first step toward that goal by taking the Pacific Division title by six games over the Portland Trail Blazers.

Magic had what had become a routinely sensational season. Despite missing 15 games with a dislocated finger, he still led the league in assists, averaging an NBA-record 13.1 per game. He also led the league's guards in field-goal accuracy (56.5) and was fifth in steals (2.24 per game). In the 67 games that he played in, he had 12 triple—doubles and 43 double—doubles. Magic's magnificent play earned him his second straight spot on the All-NBA First Team, and when the players were polled for the *Sporting News* All-NBA team, Magic was the top vote-getter.

With Magic leading the way, the Lakers swept Sacramento in the opening round of the playoff, 3–0, derailed Dallas 4–1, and powered past Phoenix in the Western finals, 4–2. Their only obstacle now was the Boston Celtics and Larry Bird. On the court the Lakers would be contesting the current Celtic players, but they would also have to battle "ghosts" and the traditions symbolized by the 14 NBA championship banners proudly hanging above the fabled parquet floor like centurions. In six championship series, the Lakers had never beaten Boston and the Celtics had *never* lost a deciding game in the Boston Garden.

The championship series created a lot of excitement throughout the country. These were easily the two best teams in basketball, two of the best ever assembled, and the two top superstars in the NBA would be facing each other in a championship for the first time since the NCAA title game five years earlier.

The Lakers thumbed their noses at the ghosts and the tradition in the first game as they beat Boston, 115–109. Incredibly, they were all poised to take the second game too, but they lost their poise and the game in overtime, 124–121. They had been leading by two points with eighteen seconds left in regulation time and had the ball in their possession. But then the Boston Garden goblins struck. Magic made a mental error, James Worthy threw a pass away, and the Celtics did the rest.

Back in the safety of the Forum, where Hollywood celebrities do the bewitching, the Lakers rebounded with a 137–104 laugher, led by Magic's specialty—a triple—double—that included a championship-round record, 21 assists. The Lakers were in command of the fourth game too, leading by five points with less than a minute left to play. But Magic made a bad pass and missed two free throws, which allowed Bird to lead the Celtics to another OT win, 129–125. The teams split the next two games, each winning at home to tie the series at 3–3; and then it was showdown time in the Chamber of Horrors, the Boston Garden.

The Celts spent most of the game building up a 14-point lead, but with just over a minute left on the clock the Lakers had whittled it down to three and were on the attack. Magic was bouncing the ball up the court, when Dennis Johnson's quick hands flashed out and slapped it away. Michael Cooper alertly recovered it, though, and passed it back to the Magician. Magic began dribbling, his eyes scanning the court, and then he spotted James Worthy all alone under the basket. But in the second it takes for a heart to break, Cedric Maxwell swiped the ball, the game, and the championship out of Magic's hands. The Lakers had lost another title to the Celtics and had allowed the 1984 NBA championship banner to become the fifteenth to hang from the rafters in Boston Garden, where the goblins perch with glee.

Magic didn't even try to sleep that night. He just sat in his Boston hotel room with his two best friends, Isiah Thomas and Mark Aguirre, listening to music and talking about anything except basketball.

The feeling was so bad for the Lakers that, according to Pat Riley, "It took us a long time to get over that loss. It took us a month into the next regular season to get over it."

But they did get over it. The Lakers began the new season with a mission. They were a team with a dream. They dedicated themselves to winning the NBA championship, and their special hope was that they would do it in Beantown. Magic, especially, felt the need to redeem himself.

The regular season and the preliminary playoff rounds—in which they swept the Suns, 3–0, pounded Portland, 4–1, and drilled Denver, 4–1—were merely a prelude. For Magic and the rest of the Lakers, the real season was just beginning.

But their opening game bombed in Boston, their mission stalled on the launching pad. The Celtics just wiped them off the polished parquet floor, 148–114, the second-worst drubbing ever in an NBA final round game. Magic was stunned. "Not in my wildest dreams, or anyone else's, did we think this would happen. We just got an old-fashioned whippin'." Kareem, who had played like the man who wasn't there, promised his teammates he would be there for the rest of the series and exhorted them to be ready too.

Kareem played up to his promise in game two. He tossed in 30 points, grabbed 17 rebounds, and passed off for eight assists, in leading the Lakers to victory. The scene shifted to the Forum for game three, but the Lakers kept their act together. They clobbered the Celtics 136–111, as Kareem poured in 26 points and snared 14 rebounds while James Worthy led the Lakers with 29 points. Game four was a classic nail-biter. The Celtics, behind the clutch shooting of Larry Bird and Danny Ainge, had battled to tie the game at 105, and they had the ball with only seconds left to play. The fans in the Forum and in front of their televisions knew that Boston would try to get the ball to Bird for the last shot. When the ball did come to Larry, Magic switched off Dennis Johnson to double-team Bird. But Bird didn't shoot; he whipped the pass over to D.J., who swished a twenty-one footer through the nets at the buzzer to give Boston the game, 107–105. After the game Magic explained why he had left his man to double-up on Bird. "Larry has beaten us so much we'd prefer someone else to take that shot. But Dennis knocked it down. I didn't think about it until the shot went in the basket. That's when it hit me—we lost!"

The Lakers had to regroup quickly. They couldn't afford to lose the fifth game at the Forum and go back to Boston needing to win both games. Magic, with 26 points and 17 assists, and Kareem, with 36 points, seven rebounds, seven assists, and three blocked shots, didn't let the Lakers Lose. "We had to win this one," Magic explained. "It was getting to where people were saying we can't win the big ones. Well, we showed them. We won it. We can win it all. We just have to put our minds to it." But that was at the Forum; now it was back to Boston Bedlam, where the ball takes funny bounces.

But this time the Lakers kept their poise, took control of the game, and conquered the Celtics, in Boston, 111–100. Kareem, still keeping his promise, put in 29 points. Worthy added 28, and Magic, who played an all-around masterful game, added a triple double to the winning equation. The ghosts in the rafters would go hungry this year.

In the winning locker room Magic sat exhausted but thrilled, a happy, sunshine smile lighting up his face. "It was a long year. Ever since they beat us here last year, we've waited for this chance. They said we couldn't win here. But we did it by outworking them, outhustling them, getting every loose ball— which we should have done last year. But no matter. We've done it now, and we've done it for all the Lakers teams of the past that were frustrated here. We had to take it to another level. We had to play on a higher level, past what we played the rest of the season and in the playoffs. In your guts you can feel it. This is what you live for."

Magic felt like a king, and he wanted the Lakers to retain the crown they had captured in Boston. They began the 1985–86 season with a rush, going 24–3, the best start in Laker history. And they just kept rolling, finishing the season with a 62–20 record. People were beginning to talk about a dynasty, talk about the Lakers being the best team ever. They had been to the finals five times in the last six years and had won the championship three times. They were the kings of the hill.

The Lakers began the playoffs in royal fashion, dispensing with the Spurs in three straight. They had to dirty their uniforms a bit against the Mavericks but beat back the pretenders, 4–2. The last obstacle on the royal road to a rematch with Boston was Houston. The Rockets dropped the first game like a subject in front of his king, but then in an abrupt about-face the Rockets revolted and swept the Lakers from their throne with four consecutive wins.

The Lakers were shocked and deeply disturbed at their sudden expulsion from the playoffs. But by the time they assembled at training camp for the 1986–87 season, they were determined to play their way back to the top. Once again they were a team on a mission, and Magic was the mission master.

The Lakers, with Magic at the point, started the season with a 24–3 surge. The Lakers kept running and winning, finishing the regular season with a league-best of 65–17 record, six games better than Boston. During training camp Pat Riley had asked Magic to score more, and he responded with a career-best 23.9 average—tenth best in the league; and he still managed to lead the league in assists, with a 12.2 average. Magic's phenomenal season earned him his first NBA Most Valuable Player award. He became only the third guard to win the award, the first since Oscar Robertson had done it in 1964. At the news conference where the award was announced, Magic was all smiles. "I'd like to thank Larry Bird [who had won the award three years running] for having a slightly off year, and I want to strangle Michael Jordan [who was the runner-up] for putting all that pressure on me." The award, which a lot of people felt was long overdue, was appreciated, but Magic was more interested in another championship ring.

The Lakers were devastating in the first three rounds of the playoffs. They won eleven of twelve games while defeating Denver, Golden State, and Seattle. They were super sensational in the wrap-up game against Seattle, trouncing the Supersonics 133–102. The Laker fast break, with Magic at the throttle, was operating at an awesome level of precision. Like a high-speed train it ran through the night past the slow trains, a blur of purple and gold.

Dick Versace, an assistant coach of the Detroit Pistons who was scouting the Lakers, was awed by their performances. "They're cosmic. They're playing better than any team I've ever seen." But the Lakers weren't going to beat Boston with press clippings. It was Show Time.

The Lakers lit up the Forum with their high-energy running

game from the opening tip-off until the final whistle blew on their 126–113 victory in the first game of the 1987 championship series. Magic, playing as though he held the ball on a string, popped for 29 points, pulled down eight boards, and handed out 13 assists, and with all that ball handling didn't commit a single turnover. It was Magical.

In game two the Lakers simply blew Boston away, 141–122. The Lakers' high-speed express was open full throttle, as Magic dealt out 20 assists while threading the net for 22 points. And Michael Cooper, who hit for 20 consecutive points, was just in another zone. Pat Riley had said, "We wanted to push it, push it, and drive it and keep doing that for as long as we could." And they did it—for the full 48 minutes.

On the jet carrying the Celtics back to Boston, one of the writers joked that it seemed to move slower than the Laker fast break. Larry Bird, though, wasn't laughing. "If this continues, maybe it's time to make some changes and get some people who will play every night."

The Boston Garden supplied the Celtics with the necessary tonic in game three, as they hung in and hung on, 109–103. It looked like the Celtics had dropped the curtain on Show Time, as they patiently built a 16-point lead in the third period of game four. But with less than half a minute to play, Magic lobbed a perfect alley-oop pass that Kareem slam-dunked to put the Lakers up by one. Bird answered back with a clutch three-pointer to give the Celts a two-point lead with only 12 seconds left. Kareem was fouled with .07 showing on the clock. He made the first one and missed the second, but the goblins must have been on a break because the rebound went out of bounds off of Boston. The pass came in to Magic, who started to take a 20-footer, but Kevin McHale jumped out at him. So Magic pulled the ball down and drove across the foul line, where he was walled off by three Lakers. He pulled up, spun left, and put up a soft "baby" sky hook that swished through the nets to give the Lakers a 107–106 win, and a 3–1 lead in the series. According to one Boston writer it was "the single most devastating loss in Celtic history."

The Lakers should have put Boston away in game five, but they let them bounce back. For most of the game it looked as though Magic, who led the Lakers with 29 points, eight boards, 12 assists, and four steals, was playing one against five. Afterward he told the team, "We can't settle for jump shots all night. We've got to create. We're just standing around and watching." He reminded them that they had to be aggressive, run the floor, drive to the hoop, and take the elbows.

But back at the Forum for game six, it was Boston who snatched a 56–51 lead at the half. In the third quarter, though, Magic took control. He ignited an 18–2 burst, including his own slam dunk that put the Lakers ahead to stay, and they cruised to a 106–83 win and the NBA championship.

Magic, who led the Lakers in scoring, rebounding, assists, and steals, and played defense like an octopus, was a unanimous choice for the Most Valuable Player award in the championship series. It made him the only person to have won it three times.

In the locker room afterward, Magic was aglow. "There's no question this is the best team I've ever played on. It's fast; it can shoot and rebound. It has everything." There is also no question that Magic was the one who made it all come together.

7

Show Time in Motown

While the Lakers were still celebrating their victory in the 1987 playoffs, Pat Riley put them in the hot seat for the upcoming season by announcing that the Lakers would repeat in 1988. Some of the Lakers wished that their coach hadn't spoken, but Magic let it be known that it was his ambition too. No team had won back to back since the Celtics had in 1968 and '69. Magic knew that for the Lakers to be considered one of the great teams of all time, they would have to repeat.

The Lakers picked up Riley's challenge in training camp and completed the season with a 62–20 record. They became the first team in history to win 60 or more games in consecutive seasons.

In the opening round of the playoffs the Spurs went quietly in three straight. But the Utah Jazz put up a fierce fight and split the first six games against the surprised Lakers. The seventh game was a Magical show. He was on top of his game—wheeling, dealing, pushing the ball up the floor, scoring 23 points and handing out sixteen assists. After the game Bob Hansen, a Utah back-courter, said, "He's the greatest guard in history."

The next series, against the Dallas Mavericks, also came down to a decisive seventh game, and once again Magic was masterful. He scored 24 points, hauled down 11 boards, and handed out 11 assists. Just as importantly, he played stopper against Roy Tarpley, a seven-footer, who had been hurting the Lakers all series. "Pat wanted to keep Tarpley under ten rebounds, and I told him the way to do that is to put me on him." Magic played him for most of the game, and Tarpley wound up with only seven boards. "Banging, bumping, physical play, that's what I like," grinned Magic.

And that's what Magic was going to get in the championship series against a new rival, the Detroit Pistons. The powerful

Pistons, led by the incomparable Isiah Thomas, were young, fast, talented, and the bullies of the NBA. Before the first game, Magic was asked how the series would affect his friendship with Isiah. "From now on we have to keep our distance. We understand that. There's no friendship now. When you're going for the championship, you take no prisoners."

But before the opening tap, in a beautiful display of friendship, the two men embraced each other. Once the game began, though, Detroit left tire marks all over the Lakers and downed them, 105–93. Pat Riley was furious. "We were playing one against nine," he hissed. Only Magic, who scored 28 points and passed for ten assists, was excluded from Riley's justified outburst.

Magic crawled out of a sickbed for the start of game two, but when it was over, it was the Pistons who were feeling poorly. Magic scored 23 points, snared seven boards, and connected for 11 assists. After the game Pat Riley saluted his star. "I don't think there's any doubt that Earvin Johnson showed the heart of a champion tonight. He was really weak, but he dug down and would not let us lose."

"I'm just glad I was able to fight through it," responded Magic. "I couldn't let the guys know how I felt. If I'm up, they're going to be up. They look up to me."

The third game was in the Silverdome, in Pontiac, Michigan. It was Magic's first playoff game in his home state, and he was spectacular in leading the Lakers to a 99–86 win. Afterward, in the locker room, while the team was enjoying the feast that Magic's mom had prepared for the team, James Worthy told reporters, "You have to keep your eyes on Magic all the time lest you get hit upside the head."

In game four it was the Pistons who did the hitting and the winning, 111–86. The Lakers were embarrassed at the score and the fact that they had let the Pistons bully them. Late in the game, when it didn't matter anymore, Magic took his frustration out on Isiah Thomas, and the two friends got into a pushing match. Pat Riley had smoke coming out of his ears. "I'm not disappointed and angry. I'm beyond that. I'm disgusted."

The Lakers played explosively at the start of game five, jumping out to a 15–2 lead. But foul troubles and poor shooting allowed Detroit back in the game, and the Pistons took it, 104–94. When Magic left the court near the end of the game, he made sure he was smiling. And he went over to each of the starters and slapped their hands as if they had just won the game. Magic was already thinking ahead to game six, and he didn't want any of the troops getting down when they were only one loss away from elimination. "The guys are not down," he explained. "They know what they have to do. But you got to make double sure." And Magic didn't make any excuses for his own poor play. "I just didn't get it done. I know what I did, so I just got to make sure it doesn't happen again. We're not out of it yet. We're still champions until we lose one more."

They didn't lose game six because they wouldn't surrender. They trailed 102–99 with only a minute left to play, but they stayed alive when Kareem hit two pressure-packed foul shots with only 14 seconds showing on the clock to give them the win, 103–102. In winning they had to overcome an awesome display of talent and courage by Isaiah Thomas, who pumped in 43 points while limping around the court on a severely sprained ankle.

There was one game left in the season—one game left for the Lakers to leave their footprints in the sands of NBA history. It was a close game until the Lakers made their first ten shots in the third quarter and opened a ten-point lead. Then they stretched their lead to 15 with only 7:27 left in the fourth quarter. But the Pistons kept pumping and closed to 106–105. The game hung in the balance as Magic spotted A.C. Green streaking toward the basket and threw a court-length pass. Green gathered the ball and put in the layup that gave the Lakers the win, 108–105. They had repeated as NBA champions.

In the Laker locker room the team whooped it up, and when a reporter asked Riley if the Lakers would repeat again, Kareem stuck a towel in his mouth before he could answer. But later Riley showed the pride he had in this team and, perhaps, his concern that their time had passed. "At the end of the game, what were we doing? We were watching a great basketball team hold on."

In the midst of the victory celebration, the victory that Magic had wanted most, the one that would, in his mind, insure the greatness of this Laker team, his thoughts were on his best friend. He explained how hard it was to play against Isaiah Thomas. "That's the most difficult thing I've ever had to go through, staying focused on what I had to do. I know Isaiah. His heart is as big as this room."

Throughout his years Magic has always shown how big his heart is too—whether it's on the court or in offering his help to others. From his days in the Boys Club to "A Midsummer Night's Magic" the all-star games that he organizes in the off-season to raise money for the United Negro College Fund, Magic is usually there, lending a helping hand. The day after the Pistons had beaten Magic up in game four, he still took the time to go to a children's hospital to spend time with a boy who was very ill and had asked to see him.

Earvin "Magic" Johnson has established himself as one of the best basketball players of all time, and one of the most enjoyable to watch—as he dribbles the ball with his right hand, using his left hand to hold off his defender, and then throws a no-look pass to James Worthy filling the lane or an alley-oop lob to Kareem for a slam dunk. As Larry Bird has said, "He's the best in the league. I'd *pay* to watch him." Bird isn't just talking about Magic's individual athletic talent; he's talking about his desire and his mental toughness, his ability to lead a team and instill his toughness in them. He's talking about the heart of a champion.

Pat Riley caught the special quality that Magic exudes in his book, *Showtime*. He told of an accidental meeting with Magic on a beach in the Bahamas. "And there was this one guy walking away from me with a gray T-shirt that was flapping in the breeze. I got a shudder. I thought, 'You know, one day he's gonna be gone forever. He's gonna walk right out of my life and the Lakers' lives and the fans' lives and that's going to be it. . . .'"

So while there's still time, don't miss the Magic of showtime.

8

It's Always Magic

Anyone who had watched the Lakers claw their way through the 1988 play-offs and just hold on against the younger, quicker, stronger Pistons realized that they might have witnessed the end of an era.

While many of the other teams in the Western Conference had grown more talented, the Lakers had only grown older.

And Kareem, once the hub of the team, would turn 42 during the '88–89 season and be making his farewell appearances in the NBA arenas that he had once ruled. But now, with both his stamina and his skills diminished by age, Pat Riley would have to find a way to keep winning while limiting the Big Fella's playing time. And he would have to pull this off without disturbing the delicate chemistry and cohesiveness that had bound the team together.

Riley was also concerned that the Lakers might be complacent, since they had reached their long-sought goal of back-to-back titles. He sensed that they would need a spark to ignite their competitive juices and maintain their position among the league's elite teams. So, needing to pull a rabbit out of a hat, Riley naturally turned to Magic.

During the summer he wrote Earvin a letter that said in part, "For us to win a championship this year, you're going to have to play like the most valuable player in the league. It will take that kind of performance to lift us up again."

And Magic responded to the challenge magnificently, finding a way to raise the level of his already exquisite game. From the opening tip-off to the season's final shot, Magic relentlessly drove himself and his teammates. And when the dust had settled, the Lakers were perched atop the Pacific Division with the best record in the Western Conference.

In the first play-off series, Magic initiated a three-game rout of the Trailblazers with a 30-point, 16-assist performance in game one. Afterward Portland coach Rich Adelman noted with admiration, "Magic's the reason they've played at such a high level. He's just determined not to let them slip."

And Magic kept the Lakers engine running smoothly in the first two games of their next series, against Seattle. After the second-game rout the Supersonics' coach, Bernie Bickerstaff, quipped, "The only safe place today was in the locker room." The Lakers slipped a gear in the third game but held on to win, 91–86, despite the fact that the usually unflappable Magic Man had his pockets picked by the Sonics press and turned the ball over nine times. "I kept saying to myself, Man, this isn't me, and that disappointment made me try to do more, and then I played even worse."

The Supersonics, encouraged by the close call and desperately attempting to stave off elimination, came out smoking in game four and built a seemingly insurmountable 41–12 lead in the second period. But Magic maintained his composure and led the Lakers to one of the most remarkable comeback wins in play-off history, 97–95. "I always felt in control," said the smiling-faced Magic Man. "This team never gets scared. We just said, Settle down, make this play and that play, and that's what we did."

The Lakers took a deep breath and then took on the Phoenix Suns, a team that had battled L.A. down to the wire in the Pacific Division. Phoenix, led by All-Star forward Tom Chambers and the Johnson duo, Kevin and Eddie, was expected to mount a serious challenge to the Lakers' reign as lords of the West. But Magic worked his wonder, and the Suns were swept aside in four straight games. The Lakers' win in the first game gave them an NBA-record ten straight play-off wins, and the sweep of the Suns made the Lakers the only team in NBA history to sweep three consecutive series. And the losing coach, Colton Fitzsimmons, knew just who to blame for the total eclipse of his Suns. "It's always Magic. He has a very nice cast of characters around him, but he's the one who makes them all look so good. He will not let them lose."

Magic had led the Lakers into the NBA finals for the eighth time, and it ranked as one of the most remarkable accomplishments in his incomparable ten-year career. But the dramatic prospect of watching the proud Lakers attempt to hold off another challenge from the surviving Pistons quickly turned into an anti-climactic event. First, Byron Scott, Magic's backcourt partner and L.A.'s second-leading scorer, suffered a hamstring injury in practice and was forced to sit out the series. And then in the third quarter of game two, Magic pulled up lame with an injury to *his* hamstring. As Magic limped around the court, clutching his leg, he cried out, "Why me? Why now, after all the hard work?" And two games later Detroit completed the four-game sweep and officially dethroned the Lakers as world champions.

But while the injury put an end to Magic's dream of a third-straight title, nothing could detract from his fierce effort and inspired performance throughout the season. Even before the series with the Pistons had begun, Magic's brilliance as both a player and team leader was rewarded when he was presented with his second Most Valuable Player award.

A lot of people thought that the award should have gone to Michael Jordan, but Isiah Thomas explained why he would vote for Magic. "The MVP depends on what you do for your team, what you do to make everybody else play better, and, above all else, whether or not you win. Who has done that better than Magic?"

Who, indeed? From high school to the NBA, no one has done it any better.

RECORD
SHEETS

Michael Jordan

University of North Carolina Record

YEAR	G.	MIN.	FGA	FGM	PCT.	FTA	FTM	PCT.	REB.	PTS.	AVG.
81-82	34	...	358	191	.534	108	78	.722	149	469	13.8
82-83	36	...	527	182	.535	167	123	.737	197	721	20.0
83-84	31	...	448	247	.551	145	113	.779	163	607	19.5
Totals	101	...	1333	720	.540	420	314	.748	509	1788	17.7

NBA REGULAR SEASON RECORD

YEAR	GP	MIN	FGM-FGA	PCT.	FTM-FTA	PCT.	OFF-DEF-TOT	AVG.	AST	PF-DQ	STL	BS	PTS.	AVG.
84-85	82	3144	837-1625	.515	630- 746	.845	167- 367- 534	6.5	481	285-4	196	69	2313	28.2
85-86	18	451	150- 328	.457	105- 125	.840	23- 41- 64	3.6	53	46-0	37	21	408	22.7
86-87	82	3281	1098-2279	.482	833- 972	.857	166- 264- 430	5.2	377	237-0	236	125	3041	37.1
87-88	82	3311	1069-1998	.535	723- 860	.841	139- 310- 449	5.5	485	270-2	259	131	2868	35.0
88-89	81	3255	966-1795	.538	674- 793	.860	149- 503- 652	8.4	650	247-2	234	64	2633	32.5
Totals	345	13442	4120-8025	.513	2965-3496	.848	644-1485-2129	6.1	2046	1085-8	962	411	11263	32.7

NBA PLAYOFF RECORD

YEAR	GP	MIN	FGM-FGA	PCT.	FTM-FTA	PCT.	OFF-DEF-TOT	AVG.	AST	PF-DQ	ST	BS	PTS.	AVG.
84-85	4	171	34- 78	.436	48- 58	.828	7- 16- 23	5.8	34	15-0	11	4	117	29.3
85-86	3	135	48- 95	.505	34- 39	.872	5- 14- 19	6.3	17	13-1	7	4	131	43.7
86-87	3	128	35- 84	.417	35- 39	.897	7- 14- 21	7.0	18	11-0	6	7	107	35.7
87-88	10	427	138-260	.530	82- 99	.868	23- 48- 71	7.1	47	38-1	24	12	363	36.3
88-89	17	718	199-390	.510	183-229	.799	26- 93-119	7.0	130	65-1	42	13	591	34.8
Totals	37	1579	454-907	.500	382-464	.823	68-185-253	6.8	246	142-3	90	40	1309	35.4

Magic Johnson

Michigan State University Record

YEAR	G.	MIN.	FGM	FGA	PCT.	FTM	FTA	PCT.	REB.	PTS.	AVG.
77-78	30	....	175	382	.458	161	205	.785	237	511	17.0
78-79	32	1159	173	370	.468	202	240	.842	234	548	17.1
Totals	62	.....	348	752	.463	363	445	.816	471	1059	17.1

NBA REGULAR SEASON RECORD

YEAR	G	MIN	FGM-FGA	PCT	3-PT	FTM-FTA	PCT	OFF	DEF	TOT	AST	PF-DQ	ST	TO	BS	PTS	AVG
79-80	77	2795	503-949	.530	7- 31	374-462	.810	166	430	596	563	218-1	197	305	41	1387	18.0
80-81	37	1371	312- 587	.531	3- 17	171-225	.760	101	219	320	317	100-0	127	143	27	798	21.6
81-82	78	2991	556-1036	.537	6- 29	329-433	.760	252	499	751	743	223-1	208	286	34	1447	18.6
82-83	79	2907	511- 933	.548	0- 21	304-380	.800	214	469	683	829	200-1	176	301	47	1326	16.8
83-84	67	2567	441- 780	.565	6- 29	290-358	.810	99	392	491	875	169-1	150	306	49	1178	17.6
84-85	77	2781	504- 899	.561	7- 37	391-464	.843	90	386	476	968	155-0	113	305	25	1406	18.3
85-86	72	2578	483- 918	.526	10- 43	378-434	.871	85	341	426	907	133-0	113	273	36	1354	18.8
86-87	80	2904	683-1308	.522	8- 39	535-631	.848	122	382	504	977	168-0	138	300	36	1909	23.9
87-88	72	2637	490- 996	.492	11- 56	417-489	.853	88	361	449	858	147-0	114	269	13	1048	19.6
88-89	77	2886	579-1137	.509	59-188	513-553	.911	111	496	607	988	172-0	138	312	22	1730	22.5
Totals	716	26417	5062-9543	.530	117-490	3702-4429	.835	1328	3975	5303	8025	1685-4	1464	2800	310	13583	18.9

NBA PLAYOFF RECORD

YEAR	G	MIN	FGM-FGA	PCT	3-PT	FTM-FTA	PCT	OFF	DEF	TOT	AST	PF-DQ	ST	TO	BS	PTS	AVG
79-80	16	658	103-199	.518	2- 8	85-106	.802	52	116	168	151	47-1	49	65	6	293	18.3
80-81	3	127	19- 49	.388	0- 0	13- 20	.650	8	33	41	21	14-1	8	11	3	51	17.0
81-82	14	562	83- 157	.529	0- 4	77- 93	.828	54	104	158	130	50-0	40	44	3	243	17.4
82-83	15	643	100- 206	.485	0- 11	68- 81	.840	51	77	128	192	49-0	34	64	12	268	17.9
83-84	21	837	151- 274	.551	0- 7	80-100	.800	26	113	139	284	71-0	42	79	20	382	18.2
84-85	19	687	116- 226	.513	1- 7	100-118	.847	19	115	134	289	48-0	32	76	1	333	17.5
85-86	14	541	110- 205	.537	0- 11	82-107	.766	21	79	100	211	43-0	27	45	1	302	21.6
86-87	18	666	146- 271	.539	2- 10	98-118	.831	28	111	139	219	37-0	31	51	7	392	21.8
87-88	24	965	169- 329	.514	7- 14	132-155	.852	32	98	130	303	61-0	34	83	4	477	19.9
88-89	14	518	85- 174	.489	10- 35	78- 86	.907	15	68	83	165	30-1	27	53	3	258	18.4
Totals	158	6204	1082-2090	.518	22-107	813-984	.826	306	914	1220	1965	450-3	324	571	63	2999	19.0

MICHAEL JORDAN—1989 PLAYOFF RECORD SHEET

Opponent	FGM-FGA	PCT	FTM-FTA	PCT	REB	ASST	STL	BS	PTS	AVG
1										
2										
3										
Totals										
1										
2										
3										
4										
5										
6										
7										
Totals										
1										
2										
3										
4										
5										
6										
7										
Totals										
1										
2										
3										
4										
5										
6										
7										
Totals										
Grand Total										

MAGIC JOHNSON—1989 PLAYOFF RECORD SHEET

Opponent	FGM-FGA	PCT	FTM-FTA	PCT	REB	ASST	STL	BS	PTS	AVG
1										
2										
3										
Totals										
1										
2										
3										
4										
5										
6										
7										
Totals										
1										
2										
3										
4										
5										
6										
7										
Totals										
1										
2										
3										
4										
5										
6										
7										
Totals										
Grand Total										

I hope that you liked this book. If you did,
you would probably like our other sports titles
by Richard J. Brenner:

Joe Montana • Jerry Rice. A double biography
of the two San Francisco 49er football superstars.
From childhood dreams to Super Bowl wins.
• Featuring 12 pages of exciting photos.

The World Series: The Great Contests. The
unique excitement of the Fall Classic is brought
to life in seven of the most thrilling contests of
all time. From Jackie Robinson and the Brooklyn
Dodgers to Dave Stewart and the Oakland A's.
• Featuring 16 pages of action-packed photos.

The Complete Super Bowl Story Games I-XXIV.
The most exciting moments in Super Bowl history
are brought to life, game-by-game.
• Featuring 16 pages of action-packed photos.
• Record Sheets for Super Bowl XXV.